SPECTRUM

Word Study and Phonics

Grade 5

Columbus, Ohio

Send all inquiries to:
School Specialty Publishing
8720 Orion Place
Columbus, OH 43240-2111

ISBN 0-7696-8425-4

2 3 4 5 6 7 8 9 10 POH 11 10 09 08 07

Table of Contents Grade 5

Chapter 1 Phonics

Table of Contents, continued

Chapter 2 Word Structure

Chapter 3 Vocabulary

Table of Contents, continued

NAME ______________________

Lesson 1.1 Hard and Soft c and g

- The letter **c** can make a hard sound, as in *corner* and *welcome*. When **c** is followed by **e**, **i**, or **y**, it can make a soft sound, as in *cider*, *celery*, and *cycle*.
- The letter **g** can make a hard sound, as in *ground* and *began*. When **g** is followed by **e**, **i**, or **y**, it can make a soft sound, as in *gerbil*, *fragile*, or *stingy*.

Read the clues below. Choose the word from the box that matches each clue. Make sure that the word has the correct hard or soft **c** or **g** sound.

cactus	cube	gaze	orange	prince	geology	grumble	fierce

1. a desert plant that can live on very little water (hard **c**) ______________
2. to look at something steadily (hard **g**) ______________
3. to complain (hard **g**) ______________
4. the study of Earth's history and structure (soft **g**) ______________
5. a member of the royal family (soft **c**) ______________
6. the name of a citrus fruit, as well as a color (soft **g**) ______________
7. a solid shape that has six sides of the same size (hard **c**) ______________
8. dangerous or savage (soft **c**) ______________

Read the words in each line below. Circle the word that has the same hard or soft **c** or **g** sound as the word in bold.

1. **police**	picnic	include	juice	golden
2. **engine**	Georgia	wagon	struggle	nighttime
3. **forgotten**	college	legend	cage	goose
4. **popcorn**	decide	candle	peace	cheerful
5. **village**	gymnastics	grounded	celery	global
6. **gravity**	weight	fragile	energy	glitter
7. **copper**	principal	cartwheel	cereal	slice

NAME ______________________________

Lesson 1.1 Hard and Soft **c** and **g**

Read the paragraphs below. Look for words with the hard and soft **c** and **g** sounds. Then, write the words in the correct columns. You do not need to list the same word more than once. Hint: Two words can be listed in more than one column.

The tea ceremony is an age-old ritual that has an important place in traditional Japanese society. The person who prepares and serves the tea is called a practitioner. Some ceremonies may last as long as four hours and include food, while other ceremonies are much shorter.

A tea practitioner may study the art of the tea ceremony for an entire lifetime. A practitioner must know the different types of tea and how they are produced. He or she must also know about other elements of Japanese culture, like kimonos, incense, and flower arranging. Even guests at a tea ceremony need to know about tea and the proper manners and gestures to use.

Certain equipment is needed for even a basic ceremony. For example, a rectangular white cloth is used to clean the tea bowl. A ladle, called *hishaku*, is used for removing tea from the pot. The tea bowls are among the most important parts of the ceremony. On some occasions, fragile bowls that are hundreds of years old may be used. Even an irregular bowl can be valuable. Its imperfections show that it was handmade.

Hard **c**	Soft **c**	Hard **g**	Soft **g**
______	______	______	______
______	______	______	______
______	______	______	______
______	______	______	______
______	______		
______	______		
______			
______			
______			
______			
______			

NAME ___________________________

Lesson 1.1 Hard and Soft c and g

Read the paragraphs below. Listen carefully to the **c** or **g** sound in each word in bold. On the line beside it, write hard **c**, hard **g**, soft **c**, or soft **g**.

The **Jungle** ________________ *Book* has been a part of many children's lives **since** ________________ it was first published in 1894. Its author, Rudyard **Kipling** ________________, was the **youngest** ________________ person ever to **receive** ________________ the Nobel Prize for Literature. Although he wrote other books and poems **during** ________________ his life, **nothing** ________________ matched the **huge** ________________ success of *The Jungle Book.*

The book **consists** ________________ of several stories which were first printed in **magazines** ________________. The main character is a boy named **Mowgli** ________________, who was raised by wolves in the jungles of India. More than a hundred years have passed since the stories' **original** ________________ **publication** ________________, but they are still enjoyed by kids all around the world.

Complete each sentence below with a word from the box. The word you choose should make sense in the sentence and have the correct sound.

African	decided	gathered	called	England

1. Rudyard Kipling was born in Bombay, India, which is ________________ (hard **c**) Mumbai today.

2. Kipling and his sister spent part of their childhood in ________________ (hard **g**).

3. After Kipling finished school, he ________________ (soft **c**) to work as a newspaper editor in India.

4. Kipling ________________ (hard **g**) the material for his book *Just So Stories for Little Children* during his ________________ (hard **c**) travels.

NAME ______________________

Lesson 1.1 Hard and Soft c and g

On the line, write the word that names the picture. Then, write the words from the box that have the same hard or soft **c** or **g** sound under the correct headings.

oxygen	Iceland	gypsy	coupon	specific	sugar	computer	griddle

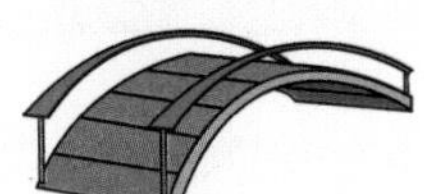

______________ ______________ ______________ ______________

______________ ______________ ______________ ______________

______________ ______________ ______________ ______________

Read the sentences below. On the line, write the word from the box that best completes each sentence. If the word contains a hard **c** or **g** sound, circle it. If it contains a soft **c** or **g** sound, underline it.

rice	gloomy	legendary	crab	grandmother's
	ingredients	gently	vegetables	spicy

1. Amelia spent the afternoon at her ______________ house.
2. It was a cold and ______________ day, but the house was warm and cozy.
3. Granny Kay stirred a pot of ______________ simmering broth.
4. "Gumbo is a hot and ______________ Louisiana soup or stew," said Granny Kay.
5. "White ______________ is one of the most important ______________ in gumbo."
6. "The secret is using the best shrimp, ______________, and crawfish."
7. "It's also important to use plenty of fresh ______________, like okra, tomatoes, bell peppers, onions, and celery."
8. Amelia tasted the gumbo from the wooden spoon. "Now I see why your recipe is so ______________ in our family!" exclaimed Amelia.

NAME ______________________

Lesson 1.2 The Sounds of s

The letter **s** can make different sounds.

- It can make the /s/ sound, as in *stranger.*
- It can make the /z/ sound, as in *busy.*
- It can make the /sh/ sound, as in *sugar* or *pressure.*
- It can make the /zh/ sound, as in *casual.*

Read the sentences below. On the line, write the **s** sound (**s**, **z**, **zh**, or **sh**) you hear in each word in bold. If the word contains more than one sound of **s**, separate the sounds with a slash. (Ex.: s/z)

1. The **Smithsonian** ______ Institution has 19 **museums** ______ and 7 research centers.
2. **Most** ______ of the **buildings** ______ are in Washington, D.C.
3. The Smithsonian **owns** ______ about 142 million **items** ______.
4. The Anacostia Museum **is** ______ a place where people can learn about African American **traditions** ______ and **history** ______.
5. The Smithsonian owns the **spacesuit** ______ Neil **Armstrong** ______ wore when he walked on the moon in 1969.
6. Two giant **pandas** ______, named *Mei Xiang* and *Tian Tian*, are on loan to the Smithsonian Zoo until 2010.
7. The National Gem and Mineral Collection **includes** ______ more than 375,000 **specimens** ______.
8. The Star of **Asia** ______ **Sapphire** ______ is one of the most famous in the collection and makes quite an **impression** ______.
9. Many people are interested in seeing **treasures** ______ like the Hope diamond—the world's **largest** ______ deep blue diamond.

NAME ____________________

Lesson 1.2 The Sounds of s

Read each word in bold below. Say the words beside it out loud to yourself. Then, circle the word that has the same sound of **s**.

1. **asleep**	measure	locksmith	music
2. **poison**	Spanish	usual	cheese
3. **casual**	pleasure	spaghetti	news
4. **expansion**	somersault	sure	deserve
5. **tension**	desert	perhaps	tissue

Complete each joke below with a word from the box. The word you choose should make sense in the sentence and have the correct sound of **s**.

treasure	spare	sugarcane	listening	cards	dries	silence

1. **Q:** What has six legs, three ears, four tusks, and two trunks?

   A: An elephant with ____________________ parts (/s/ sound).

2. **Q:** Where do frogs keep their ____________________ (/zh/ sound)?

   A: In a croak of gold at the end of the rainbow.

3. **Q:** What gets wetter the more it ____________________ (/z/ sound)?

   A: A towel.

4. **Q:** How do you stop a charging elephant?

   A: Take away its credit ____________________ (/z/ sound).

5. **Q:** What is so fragile that even saying its name can break it?

   A: ____________________ (/s/ sound).

6. **Q:** Why does history keep repeating itself?

   A: Because we weren't ____________________ (/s/ sound) the first time.

7. **Q:** What does the candyman use to help him walk?

   A: A ____________________ (/sh/ sound).

NAME ____________________

Review Hard and Soft **c** and **g** and the Sounds of **s**

Read the clues below. On the line, write the word from the box that matches the clue and has the sound listed in parentheses. Then, find each word in the word search puzzle.

government	speechless	Georgia	tease	unusual
positive	cellar	insurance	picnic	fragile

1. unique; the opposite of common (/zh/ sound) ____________________
2. a type of basement (soft **c**) ____________________
3. delicate; easily damaged (soft **g**) ____________________
4. protection against loss from fire or theft (/sh/ sound) ____________________
5. a southern state (soft **g**) ____________________
6. a political body that directs the affairs of a country (hard **g**) ____________________
7. a meal that is eaten outside (hard **c**) ____________________
8. to poke fun at (/z/ sound) ____________________
9. to be unable to speak, often because of surprise (/s/ sound) ____________________
10. the opposite of *negative* (/z/ sound) ____________________

n	k	e	t	y	m	m	f	t	n	g	u	a	a	e
m	l	o	e	r	n	p	v	c	y	s	n	q	w	c
j	i	f	r	a	g	i	l	e	g	t	u	c	i	o
l	p	s	p	e	e	c	h	l	e	s	s	v	n	a
q	f	t	o	b	o	n	d	l	e	x	u	h	s	p
t	e	a	s	e	r	i	b	a	r	v	a	f	u	i
n	k	f	i	r	g	c	b	r	z	e	l	g	r	y
j	u	w	t	p	i	g	q	w	a	p	o	g	a	t
n	u	r	i	t	a	n	w	e	u	u	k	l	n	d
h	g	o	v	e	r	n	m	e	n	t	e	r	c	v
j	y	b	e	d	s	r	t	k	c	l	s	n	e	p

NAME ______________________

Review Hard and Soft **c** and **g** and the Sounds of **s**

Read the words in the box. Write each word under the correct heading below.

clasped	pleasant	sure	casual	always	decision	springtime	measure
costly	misplace	wisdom	sugar	rosy	expansion	leisure	pressure

/s/ sound	/z/ sound	/zh/ sound	/sh/ sound
______	______	______	______
______	______	______	______
______	______	______	______
______	______	______	______

REVIEW: CHAPTER 1 LESSONS 1–3

Circle the word in parentheses that best completes each sentence below. On the line, write the sound of **c** or **g** that appears in the word.

1. The word *castle* (originally, usually) came from a Latin word meaning *fortress.* ______
2. Throughout history, castles have been used as protection against enemies, as well as homes for their owners in times of (place, peace). ______
3. Most castles included features that were intended to (crowd, protect) the occupants. ______
4. For example, a moat was a (large, gentle), deep trench filled with water that surrounded a castle. ______
5. Moats were difficult for enemies to cross, and they also made it difficult for enemies to dig (underground, grateful) tunnels to the castle. ______
6. A (legend, drawbridge) could help the owner of a castle control who entered and exited the castle. ______
7. Castles built in enemy territory could be used to take over the (amazing, surrounding) area. ______

NAME ____________________

Lesson 1.3 Consonant Digraphs

A **digraph** is a blend of two consonants that form a new sound.
- The digraph **sh** makes the /sh/ sound, as in ***sh**ovel* and *sma**sh***.
- The digraph **ch** can make the /ch/ sound, as in ***ch**oose* and *lun**ch***. It can also make the /k/ sound, as in ***ch**ord*, and the /sh/ sound, as in ***ch**ef*.

Read the letter below. Underline the words that contain the digraphs **sh** or **ch**. Then, write each underlined word below the correct heading. You do not need to list the same word more than once.

Dear Shelby,

Are you having a good spring break? My visit to Chicago has been excellent so far. Uncle Chris is a chef at a chic restaurant. He's also a member of a choir. We ate at his restaurant one night, and I chose a delicious shellfish dish. Aunt Charlotte is a chemist. She spends most of her time doing research.

My cousin, Charley, is quite a character. If he lived closer, I have a hunch you two would become friends in no time. He seemed shy at first, but he turned out to have such a great sense of humor. Charley is a champion chess player. He also raises chameleons and has a shaggy sheepdog named Harold.

See you soon!

Maggie

/sh/ sound		/ch/ sound	/k/ sound
______	______	______	______
______	______	______	______
______	______	______	______
______	______	______	______
______		______	______
______		______	
______		______	

NAME ______________________

Lesson 1.3 Consonant Digraphs

- The digraph **th** can make the unvoiced /th/ sound, as in ***th**imble* and *me**th**od*. It can also make the voiced /th/ sound in ***th**ough* and *wea**th**er*.
- The digraph **wh** can make the /hw/ sound, as in ***wh**isker* and ***wh**en*. It can also make the /h/ sound, as in ***wh**o* and ***wh**ole*.
- The digraph **ph** makes the /f/ sound, as in ***ph**oto* and *trium**ph***.

Read each word in bold below. Circle the digraph. On the line, write the letter of the word beside it that has the same sound as the digraph.

1. ______ **thousand** a. breathe b. ruthless c. those
2. ______ **wheat** a. whole b. whoever c. whine
3. ______ **pharmacy** a. fuel b. patterns c. pathway
4. ______ **thicken** a. tollbooth b. them c. gather
5. ______ **whimper** a. hurray b. whose c. whistle
6. ______ **another** a. thunder b. feather c. washcloth

Draw a line to match each word with its definition. Then, think of another word that contains the same digraph sound and write it on the line.

1. ______________	mother	the location where one was born
2. ______________	Philadelphia	the opposite of *half*
3. ______________	birthplace	a place that sells medical prescriptions
4. ______________	thoughtless	between twelfth and fourteenth
5. ______________	photograph	a device used for taking a temperature
6. ______________	thermometer	the largest city in Pennsylvania
7. ______________	whole	without thought
8. ______________	pharmacy	a female parent
9. ______________	thirteenth	an image created with a camera

NAME ______________________________

Lesson 1.4 More Consonant Digraphs

The digraphs **ck**, **ng**, and **gh** can come in the middle or at the end of a word.

- The digraph **ck** makes the /k/ sound, as in *smack* and *hockey*.
- The digraph **ng** makes the /ng/ sound, as in *earring* and *finger*.
- The digraph **gh** can make the /f/ sound, as in *rough* and *laughing*.

Read the paragraphs below. On each line, write the digraph (**ck**, **ng**, or **gh**) that correctly completes the word.

On a sunny Saturday afternoon, Ja_____ Kimble met Captain Morales at the airplane ha_____ar. The you_____ pilot gave his newest student a cheerful greeti_____. He put on a cra_____ed, worn leather ja_____et and a baseball hat.

"This must be rou_____ for you," Captain Morales said knowi_____ly. He grabbed a set of keys from an inside po_____et in his jacket. He and Jack entered the co_____pit and strapped themselves in. "What made you decide to learn how to fly?" he inquired.

"I guess I had finally had enou_____," replied Jack. "Bei_____ terrified of flyi_____ was starti_____ to interfere with my life. I didn't want to let my fear control me any lo_____er," he admitted.

"Tackli_____ your fears takes a lot of stre_____th," said the captain. "But I guarantee it will make you a tou_____er, stro_____er person."

Jack chu_____led. "That's what I'm hopi_____!" he exclaimed.

"You're on the right tra_____," said Captain Morales as he che_____ed his headphones and adjusted some switches on the control panel. "Sti_____ with me, and you'll be flying in no time."

NAME ______________________________

Lesson 1.4 More Consonant Digraphs

Complete each sentence with a word from the box and circle the digraph.

longer	hungry	sitting	lightning	sipping	block	thinking	enough

1. ____________________ on porches and ____________________ iced-tea is a neighborhood tradition on Ella's ____________________.
2. On stormy summer evenings, when ____________________ streaks the sky, Ella and her brothers sit at the kitchen table and play cards.
3. Just ____________________ about summer makes Ella ____________________ for fresh strawberries.
4. She can't get ____________________ of all the things that make up lazy summer days.
5. When the days get shorter and the nights get ____________________, Ella begins storing up her summer memories.

Each picture below has a rhyming word in the box. Write the rhyming word on the first line. Then, think of another rhyming word that contains the same consonant digraph and write it on the second line.

wing	packet	clearing	block	tongue

1. ____________________ ____________________
2. ____________________ ____________________
3. 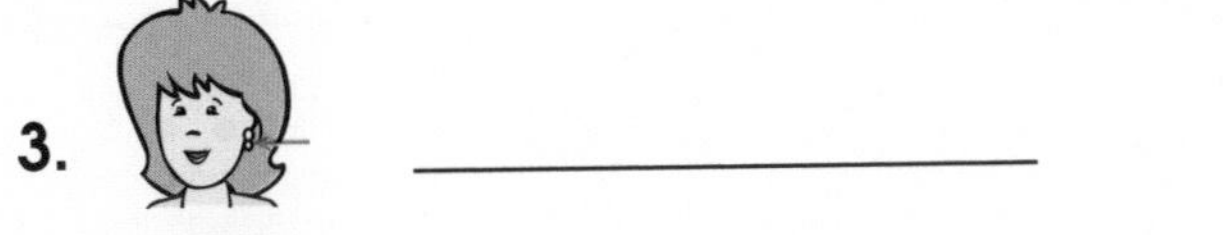 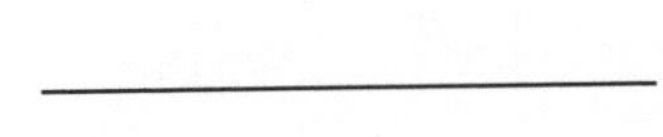 ____________________ ____________________
4. 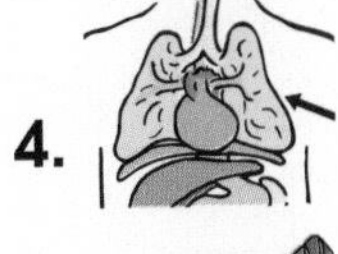 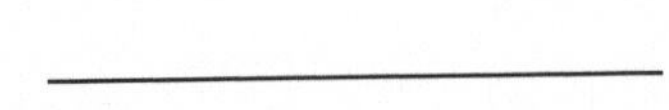 ____________________ ____________________
5.  ____________________ ____________________

NAME ______________________________

Lesson 1.5 Silent Consonants

In some consonant pairs, one letter is silent.
- The letters **kn** can make the /n/ sound, as in ***kn**uckle*. The **k** is silent.
- The letters **wr** can make the /r/ sound, as in ***wr**inkle*. The **w** is silent.
- The letters **sc** can make the /s/ sound, as in ***sc**enery*. The **c** is silent.
- The letters **mb** can make the /m/ sound, as in *li**mb***. The **b** is silent.

Read the sentences below. In each sentence, circle the word or words that contain a silent consonant pair. Make a slash (/) through each silent letter.

1. Although his knee hurt badly, Ryan climbed to the summit of the mountain and gazed in awe at the spectacular scenery.
2. Your science book is in your knapsack, the scissors are in the desk drawer, and the wrench is in the shed.
3. When Logan was wrestling with his brother, he scraped the knuckles on his left hand and sprained his thumb.
4. The puppy wriggled and writhed in excitement when he smelled his owner's scent through the open window.

Read each clue below. The word that matches the clue is written in bold beside it, but the letters are scrambled. Unscramble the letters, and write the word on the line. Hint: Each word will contain a silent consonant pair.

1. I have a sharp blade and am used for cutting or slicing. **nekif** ____________________
2. I am part of your body, like an arm or a leg. I can also be used to refer to a branch of a tree. **blmi** ____________________
3. I am the first digit on the human hand. **tbhmu** ____________________
4. I am a homophone for *rap*. **wpar** ____________________
5. I am the noise made by tapping knuckles against a door. **ocknk** ____________________

NAME ______________________

Lesson 1.5 Silent Consonants

Read each word in bold below and circle the silent consonant pair. On the line, write the letter of the word that contains the same silent consonant pair.

1. ______	**kneel**	**a.** nearby	**b.** knuckle	**c.** kennel
2. ______	**wrapper**	**a.** wooden	**b.** replacement	**c.** wrestle
3. ______	**combing**	**a.** tomb	**b.** boom	**c.** tumble
4. ______	**wrath**	**a.** wiry	**b.** writing	**c.** rattle
5. ______	**knob**	**a.** knighthood	**b.** keepsake	**c.** naughty
6. ______	**wren**	**a.** worried	**b.** wring	**c.** wart
7. ______	**crumbs**	**a.** crabby	**b.** dumber	**c.** murmur

Fill in the blank in each sentence below with a word from the box. Circle the silent letter in the word.

wriggling	scientist	thumb	wreath	scenery	scissors	knead	wring

1. Marie Curie was a ____________________ who was known for her work with radiation.
2. If you ____________________ out the wet towels before you hang them on the clothesline, they will dry much more quickly.
3. Rosie and Daniel helped paint the ____________________ for the play.
4. The robin hungrily watched the fat worm ____________________ out of its hole.
5. In the famous nursery rhyme, Little Jack Horner put his ____________________ into a pie and pulled out a plum.
6. Use a pair of ____________________ to cut out the article in the newspaper.
7. Grandma made a ____________________ to hang on the front door.
8. You must ____________________ the bread dough and then let it rise for an hour.

NAME ______________________

Lesson 1.6 More Silent Consonants

When two or three consonants appear together, one letter is sometimes silent.

- The letters **gn** can make the /n/ sound, as in *desi**gn***. The **g** is silent.
- The letters **dg** can make the /j/ sound, as in *lo**dg**e*. The **d** is silent.
- The letters **rh** can make the /r/ sound, as in ***rh**yme*. The **h** is silent.
- The letters **tch** can make the /ch/ sound, as in *fe**tch***. The **t** is silent.
- The letters **gh** can be silent, as in *mi**gh**t* and *hi**gh***.

Read the clues below. Choose the word from the box that matches each clue. Write the answers in the numbered spaces in the crossword puzzle.

hopscotch	rhinoceros	fudge	hedgehog	
gnome	twilight	pitcher	gnarl	rhyme

Across

1. the person who throws the ball to the batter in a baseball game
5. a horned African mammal
6. a small animal with a spiny back
7. a game played outside; the board is often drawn with chalk

Down

2. another word for *dusk*
3. a small creature in legends
4. a rich, sweet candy, often made with chocolate
5. two words with the same ending sound

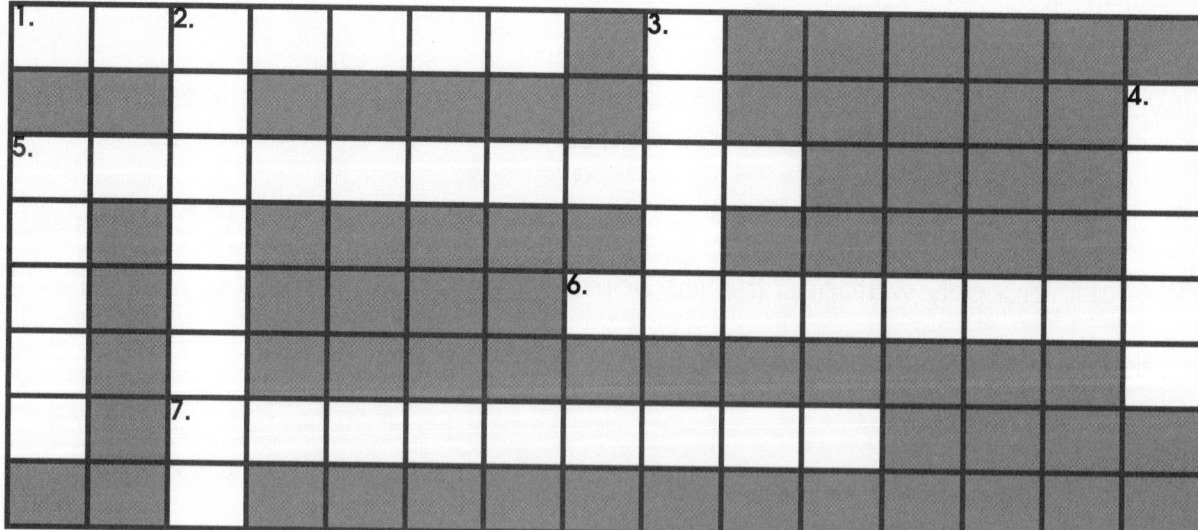

NAME ____________________

Lesson 1.6 More Silent Consonants

Every day, Alexandra jots down a few notes in her calendar about her day. Read the entries below and underline the 21 words that contain one of these silent letter combinations: **gn**, **dg**, **rh**, **tch**, or **gh**. Circle the silent letters.

May 18:	Grandpa brought over his famous rhubarb-apple pie. Ate two pieces for dessert with a wedge of sharp cheddar cheese. Yum!
May 19:	Everyone wrote their own "pledge to live by" at today's Girl Scout meeting.
May 20:	Judge Wang asked if I'd be interested in pet-sitting Wilbur and Peanut next weekend. Said yes, but I'll have to check with Mom first.
May 22:	Tierra is sleeping over tonight. Dad says we can stay up until midnight as long as we're not grouchy tomorrow.
May 24:	Aunt Jana lent me a gorgeous shimmery rhinestone necklace to wear in the play. Hope I don't get stage fright!
May 25:	Sam and his family are moving to Rhode Island as soon as school lets out for the summer. I am in shock. Who will listen to all my stories?
May 26:	Helped Ms. Weiss design and post signs for the annual school bake sale. Remember to ask Sam if he wants to make a few batches of fudge with me this weekend.
May 27:	Forgot my backpack this morning. Missed the bus and had to trudge home in the rain to get it. Delightful. What a day.
May 29:	The gnats have been really bad this spring. Saw swarms of them by the hedge in the front yard. Ask Dad if they bite.
May 30:	Brought a sketchpad to the farmers' market. I think Mr. Lilo is going to be really proud of the progress I made.
May 31:	Lightning hit the Morettis' pine tree last night. Luckily, the biggest branches that came down didn't do any damage. Close call, though!

NAME ______________________

Lesson 1.7 The Sound of Ti and Ci

The letters **ti** and **ci** can stand for the /sh/ sound, as in *descrip**tio**n* and *pre**cio**us.*

Read the sentences below. Fill in each blank with the letters **ti** or **ci**. If you are not sure about the correct spelling of a word, use a dictionary.

1. Money means different things to different people. Most people would agree that money's benefits are what makes it valuable and spe______al.
2. Some people are very cau______ous with their money, and others pay less atten______on to how it is spent.
3. Because earning an income requires lots of time and effort, most people have learned to appre______ate the value of a dollar.
4. Commer______als are everywhere, and their job is to make consumers believe that they need the product a corpora______on or company is selling.
5. A careful investiga______on will lead you to see you don't actually need most products that are advertised.
6. The sugges______ons of experts show that dividing your money into three categories can be a wise idea.
7. Some money should be set aside for spending on fun and recrea______on, like admission to a movie or a present for a friend.
8. A por______on of your money should be put in a savings account where it can grow over time and be used for something important, like your educa______on.
9. Finally, some people like to make a dona______on to a charity or a cause they think is espe______ally worthwhile.
10. Whether it is your ambi______on to become a physi______an, a musi______an, or a beauti______an, you have plenty of time to figure out what money means to you and how you choose to manage it.

NAME ______________________________

Lesson 1.7 The Sound of **Ti** and **Ci**

Read each definition below. On the line, write the letter of the word that matches the definition.

1. ______ a person who is under a doctor's care	**a.** abbreviation
2. ______ fake or phony	**b.** precious
3. ______ priceless or very valuable	**c.** politician
4. ______ fierce or savage	**d.** patient
5. ______ extremely old	**e.** artificial
6. ______ the pictures or images in a book	**f.** vicious
7. ______ a slow-moving mass of ice	**g.** ancient
8. ______ a person who holds a government office	**h.** illustrations
9. ______ a shortened way of writing something	**i.** glacier

On the line, write the word from the box that best completes each sentence below.

ancient	addition	electrician	Martians	official
multiplication	magician	subtraction	Egyptian	

1. A person who pulls a rabbit out of an empty hat is a ____________________.
2. ____________________, ____________________, ____________________, and division are the four basic math processes.
3. The ____________________ pyramids are believed to be one of the wonders of the ____________________ world.
4. When the lights in your house aren't working, it's best to call an ____________________.
5. Do you think that scientists will one day discover ____________________ on Mars?
6. The ____________________ symbol of the Olympic Games is five intertwined rings.

NAME ______________________________

Review Digraphs, Silent Consonants, Ti and Ci

Use the following table to help you remember the different digraph sounds.

sh: /sh/ sound	**ck**: /k/ sound	**ng**: /ng/ sound
gh: /f/ sound	**wh**: /hw/ sound, /h/ sound	**ph**: /f/ sound
th: /th/ sound, /th/ sound	**ch**: /ch/ sound, /k/ sound, /sh/ sound	

REVIEW: CHAPTER 1 LESSONS 3–7

Read the passage below. Each word in bold contains a digraph. Circle the digraph and write the sound it makes on the line.

Some Native Americans, like the **Chippewa** ____________________ and the Cherokee make dreamcatchers. **According** ____________________ to cultural beliefs, bad dreams would be caught in the dreamcatcher's **webbing** ____________________.

- Gather a piece of heavy paper, like **cardstock** ____________________; string or twine; beads and **feathers** ____________________; scissors; and a hole punch.
- Cut out a **9-inch** ____________________ circle from the paper. Cut an 8-inch circle inside the larger circle, leaving you with a **ring** ____________________ of paper about 1-inch wide.
- Use the hole punch to make 15 holes around the ring. **Push** ____________________ the string **through** ____________________ one of the holes. Continue doing this in a random pattern to make a web. **When** ____________________ you have filled all the holes, tie the ends of the string together.
- Cut **another** ____________________ piece of string about 8-inches long. Tie it to the bottom of the dreamcatcher. **Pick** ____________________ out several pretty beads, and **string** ____________________ the beads and the feather onto this piece. Knot the string.
- Hang the dreamcatcher above your bed and let it protect you from bad dreams.

NAME ______________________

Review Digraphs, Silent Consonants, **Ti** and **Ci**

Read each word below. Find a rhyming word in the box and write it on the line. Then, cross out the silent letter or letters.

scene	gnome	knuckle	lodge	wrist	sign
rhyme	wreath	thumb	stitch	knowledge	thigh

1. roam ______________
2. some ______________
3. college ______________
4. which ______________
5. grime ______________
6. sly ______________
7. fine ______________
8. dodge ______________
9. teeth ______________
10. green ______________
11. buckle ______________
12. kissed ______________

REVIEW: CHAPTER 1 LESSONS 3–7

Read each clue below. Unscramble the letters beside it to find the word that matches the clue. Write the word on the line. Hint: Each word will contain the /sh/ sound spelled **ti** or **ci**.

1. a person who performs magic tricks **imcaigna** ______________
2. a book containing words and definitions **tiorydinac** ______________
3. instructions to get from one place to another **nsdictreio** ______________
4. an explosion, like that of a volcano **etirupon** ______________
5. not real; fake or phony **ificartial** ______________
6. unique; different **ascipel** ______________
7. the meaning of a word **ideinonfti** ______________
8. an advertisement seen on TV **cicoermmal** ______________
9. tasty; yummy **iioucdels** ______________
10. part of a whole, like one-third **afcrtoin** ______________

NAME ____________________

Lesson 1.8 Vowel Sounds (**ai**, **ay**, **ei**, **ey**)

The vowel pairs **ai**, **ay**, **ei**, and **ey** can make the long **a** sound, as in *sn**ai**l*, *displ**ay***, ***ei**ght*, and *th**ey***.

Read each clue. Choose the word from the box that matches the clue and write it on the line. Circle the letters in the word that make the long **a** sound.

hail	Norway	obey	reins	sleigh

1. hard icy pellets that fall from the sky ____________
2. a homophone for *rains* ____________
3. a Scandinavian country bordered by Sweden and Finland ____________
4. a vehicle pulled by horses over snow ____________
5. to do what one is told to do ____________

Underline the 11 words that contain the long **a** sound spelled **ai**, **ay**, **ei**, and **ey**. You do not need to underline the same word more than once.

A mermaid is a legendary creature who is a woman from the waist up but has a fish's tail. The earliest stories about mermaids are more than 3,000 years old. They appear in African stories as Mami Wata, in Scottish and Irish culture as merrows, and in Greek myths as oceanids or sirens.

Hans Christian Andersen's fairy tale *The Little Mermaid* was written in 1836, but it still entertains children today. You may have even seen movies or plays based on this classic. Mermaid stories often involve a romance between a human and a mermaid. The mermaid may wish to become human, but she will always be tied to the sea.

Mermaids don't really exist, but they remain an important part of storytelling culture. People can't help wanting to believe that human neighbors could live in the seas.

NAME ______________________________

Lesson 1.8 Vowel Sounds (**ai**, **ay**, **ei**, **ey**)

Read each sentence and the word in bold that follows. Circle the word from the sentence that has the same long **a** spelling as the word in bold.

1. Louis Braille invented a system of dots that allowed blind people to "read" using their fingers. (**faint**)
2. Band-Aids, or bandages with adhesive, were created by Earle Dickson for his wife, who had many small accidents in the kitchen. (**remain**)
3. James Naismith invented the game of basketball in 1891, and the first public game was played in Massachusetts in 1892. (**birthday**)
4. Blue jeans, created by Levi Strauss, were originally called *waist overalls.* (**explain**)
5. It may seem strange, but the can opener was invented 50 years after the invention of the metal can. (**hallway**)
6. Before George Washington Carver came up with many inventions using agricultural products, the main crop in the American South was cotton. (**afraid**)
7. The first Ferris wheel was invented by a bridge builder and weighed more than 4,000 tons. (**beige**)
8. Ruth Wakefield invented chocolate chips by accident. She made cookies using pieces of a semi-sweet chocolate bar and liked the way they softened without melting. (**prey**)
9. Crayons were invented by the owners of a paint company in New York City. (**subway**)
10. James Ritty, a businessman in Dayton, Ohio, invented and patented the cash register in 1879. (**sway**)
11. Henry Ford was the first person to use an assembly line that was based on conveyer belts. (**survey**)

NAME ______________________

Lesson 1.9 Vowel Sounds (**ee**, **ea**, **ie**, **ey**)

The letters **ee**, **ea**, **ie**, and **ey** can make the long **e** sound you hear in *fr**ee**ze*, *cr**ea**se*, *sh**ie**ld*, and *kidn**ey***.

Read the words below. Circle the letter of the word or words in each set that have a long **e** sound.

1. a. second	**b.** refugee	**c.** flea	**d.** windshield
2. a. mislead	**b.** bumblebee	**c.** trolley	**d.** wrench
3. a. carefree	**b.** cried	**c.** hockey	**d.** streak
4. a. nutshell	**b.** stream	**c.** confide	**d.** agreed
5. a. proceed	**b.** defense	**c.** disbelief	**d.** decrease

Write the name of each picture below on the first line. Then, write the words from the box under the heading with the same long **e** spelling.

medley	sneezing	succeed	relief	squeal	hairpiece	attorney	sunbeam

________	________	________	________
________	________	________	________
________	________	________	________

Circle the word that has the same long vowel sound as the word in bold.

1. piece	movie	qualifies	nonsense
2. barley	fireside	windshield	cement
3. heave	instead	accept	nominee
4. employee	sneak	terrified	context

NAME ______________________________

Lesson 1.9 Vowel Sounds (**ee**, **ea**, **ie**, **ey**)

Read the recipe below. On each line, write the correct long **e** spelling (**ee**, **ea**, **ie**, or **ey**) to complete the word.

Firehouse Chili

2 t______spoons olive oil

1 medium onion

1 medium red bell pepper

1 medium gr______n bell pepper

2 stalks of celery

1 pound ground turk______

4 cloves of garlic

3 tablespoons chili powder

1 teaspoon salt

2 cans diced tomatoes

2 cans kidn______ beans, drained

- Chop the onion and stalks of celery into small p______ces. Dice the peppers after removing the s______ds.
- H______t the oil in a large pot. Add the onion, peppers, celery, and turkey. Cook until the vegetables are tender and the m______t is no longer pink. If the turkey s______ms gr______sy, ask an adult to help drain the fat.
- P______l the cloves of garlic and mince them finely. Add the garlic, chili powder, and salt to the pot. Stir and continue cooking for about one minute. Add the tomatoes and b______ns. Stir and cover the pot.
- Let the chili boil br______fly, then reduce the heat and simmer for 20 minutes.
- Serve the chili with shredded ch______se, sour cr______m, chopped scallions, hearty wh______t bread, or nacho chips. It is guarant______d to be a hit!

* Remember, you always n______d to ask an adult for help in the kitchen when using knives or the stove.

NAME ______________________________

Lesson 1.10 Vowel Sounds (ind, ild, igh)

The vowel **i** can make a long sound when followed by **nd**, **ld**, or **gh**, as in *behi**nd***, *mi**ld***, and *dayli**gh**t*.

Make a check mark (✓) on the line next to the word that has the same long vowel sound as the word in bold.

1. On Saturday **night**, Liz and Alex made a special dinner for their parents.

   ______ field ______ valentine ______ eight

2. Alex used a favorite recipe from his mother's **childhood**.

   ______ weigh ______ gelatin ______ impolite

3. They were able to **find** all the ingredients at the grocery store.

   ______ copyright ______ remain ______ outfit

4. Mrs. Pavlova threatened to come into the kitchen when she heard the **wild** sounds of a food fight.

   ______ transmit ______ provide ______ soil

5. "You promised we could have the kitchen to ourselves to finish the surprise," Liz **reminded** her mom.

   ______ hind ______ grief ______ twitch

6. In just a few minutes, the mess in the kitchen was hidden out of **sight**.

   ______ footprint ______ obtain ______ combine

7. Mr. and Mrs. Palova dined by **candlelight**.

   ______ unwind ______ retail ______ stink

8. "Who was the **mastermind** behind this plan?" asked Mr. Palova.

   ______ handkerchief ______ eyesight ______ drawstring

9. Liz and Alex were **delighted** with how their surprise turned out.

   ______ blind ______ strain ______ coiled

NAME ______________________________

Lesson 1.10 Vowel Sounds (**ind**, **ild**, **igh**)

Read each clue below. On the line, write the letter of the matching word.

1. ______ an antonym for *spicy*	**a.** airtight
2. ______ a traffic signal that changes color	**b.** childhood
3. ______ a synonym for *mean*	**c.** unkind
4. ______ unable to see	**d.** stoplight
5. ______ the early part of a person's life	**e.** wild
6. ______ sealed well	**f.** wind
7. ______ to turn or tighten (a watch, for example)	**g.** colorblind
8. ______ unable to see certain colors	**h.** mild
9. ______ an antonym for *tame*	**i.** blind

Read the sentences below. On each line, write the word from the box that best completes the sentence. Circle the **ind**, **ild**, or **igh** combination that indicates the /i/ sound is long.

blindness	rind	eyesight	hind	daylight	grinding	mild

1. Muffy hurt her ____________________ leg when it got caught in a hole in the yard.

2. ____________________ savings time, when we "lose" an hour, usually begins on the last Sunday in March or the first Sunday in April.

3. Save the ____________________ from that lemon to use in the iced tea.

4. If you have a stomachache, it is best to eat bland, ____________________ foods.

5. The Inuit people wear special goggles to protect them from snow ____________________, a result of the sun's reflection on bright white snow.

6. Juliet has to wear a mouth guard at night, which keeps her from ____________________ her teeth while she sleeps.

7. After having laser surgery, Ramona's ____________________ is 20/20.

NAME ____________________

Lesson 1.11 Vowel Sounds (**oa**, **ow**, **old**, **oll**, **ost**)

- The letters **oa** and **ow** can make the long **o** sound, as in *go**a**l* and *sho**w**n*.
- The vowel **o** can make a long sound when followed by **ld**, **ll**, and **st**, as in *sco**ld***, *po**ll***, and *po**st***.

Read the paragraphs below. Circle the 13 words that have the long **o** sound spelled **oa**, **ow**, **old**, **oll**, or **ost**. Do not circle the same word more than once.

Have you every moaned and groaned about an item of clothing you've had to wear? Maybe you wear a uniform to school or dislike having to wear a fancy dress or a suit and tie for special occasions. There is no doubt, however, that clothes have grown more comfortable and more practical over the years.

During the 1500s through the 1800s, women often wore petticoats below their skirts. They were used for warmth in cold weather, but they also gave the wearer a fashionable shape. Layers and layers of fabric may have looked nice, but they didn't make movement very easy. It would have been almost impossible to run and play dressed in fashions of the time.

The corset was an uncomfortable but widely-used piece of clothing. Both women and men wore corsets, though they were most often worn by women. They squeezed a person's body into a slim shape. A tightly-laced corset could make it difficult to take a deep breath!

The cloak was a much more comfortable garment. Historians believe that cloaks have existed nearly as long as humans have. Cloaks generally close at the neck and flow loosely to the mid-calf or ankle. A woman going to the opera might fasten her cloak with a valuable gold broach. But a cloak could also be worn to protect from wind or rain during a simple morning stroll. Luckily, times have changed. There is much more flexibility about what people, especially women, can wear. Today, people can express themselves through their wardrobe, or they can simply wear what feels good.

NAME ______________________

Lesson 1.11 Vowel Sounds (**oa**, **ow**, **old**, **oll**, **ost**)

Read the clues below. On the line, write the word from the box that matches the clue. Then, circle each word in the word search puzzle.

scold	charcoal	poll	billfold	outgrow
raincoat	stagecoach	coast	crow	rowboat

1. a jacket worn in stormy weather ______________
2. a survey of what people think about a specific issue ______________
3. land that is located beside water, especially the ocean ______________
4. a synonym for *wallet* ______________
5. a large, very intelligent black bird ______________
6. a carriage drawn by horses; an old-fashioned form travel ______________
7. to speak angrily to someone ______________
8. small pieces of black material, often used as fuel in a grill ______________
9. to become too big for something ______________
10. a small water vehicle that is moved by oars ______________

s	c	o	l	d	g	e	p	o	l	l	w	v	n	i
j	t	m	c	v	a	r	r	n	p	m	o	f	d	c
o	b	l	n	s	t	a	g	e	c	o	a	c	h	b
u	t	d	q	m	o	i	b	s	j	x	q	h	i	l
t	h	r	e	y	o	n	n	m	w	t	e	a	y	c
g	d	f	r	t	h	c	q	z	b	y	c	r	o	w
r	b	i	l	l	f	o	l	d	g	t	r	c	n	p
o	o	n	b	g	e	a	w	r	n	s	k	o	l	p
w	i	b	l	l	v	t	t	y	d	c	o	a	s	t
h	a	o	b	n	r	o	w	b	o	a	t	l	v	i

NAME ______________________________

Review Vowel Sounds

Read the paragraphs below. On each line, write the letters that correctly complete the word. The words in parentheses will tell you which vowel sound the word should contain.

When m______ (long **o**) people think of a school, th______ (long **a**) picture a large building with different classrooms for ______ch (long **e**) grade level. Gold Cr______k (long **e**) School, in Gold Creek, Montana, doesn't fit that image. Gold Creek is one of about 400 one-room schoolhouses rem______ning (long **a**) in the United States. The town, like the school, is small. It does not have any stores or even a gas station. Six children attend school at the ______-fashioned (long **o**) schoolhouse, and each one is in a different grade.

As you m______t (long **i**) guess, this creates some challenges for the t______cher (long **e**). However, she has learned how to work with students at many levels. Every d______, (long **a**) she manages to cover all the subjects with each of her six students.

Things weren't alw______s (long **a**) so quiet in this western town. The first g______ (long **o**) in Montana was discovered there in the mid-1800s. This brought a wave of miners who made the journ______ (long **e**) west, hoping to strike it rich. Things change, however, and this once busy town has gone through some hard times. The residents of Gold Creek kn______ (long **o**) that if they can find a way to keep their young people close to home, the town—and the qu______nt (long **a**) little schoolhouse—still have a chance to survive.

REVIEW: CHAPTER 1 LESSONS 8–11

NAME ____________________

Review Vowel Sounds

Read the directions below. On the line next to the words in bold, write the long vowel sound you hear (**a**, **e**, **i**, or **o**) when you say the word out loud to yourself.

Hi Jing,

I've jotted down some directions from your house to mine. I hope you'll make it to the party on **Saturday** _____ with no problem. **Please** _____ feel free to call if you get lost. See you then!

Whitney _____

- Turn left on **Dovetail** _____ Lane. In about **three** _____ miles, you'll **reach** _____ the intersection of **Leaf** _____ Avenue and Willington **Road** _____. Make another left turn, and continue going **straight** _____ for about a mile.
- The last two buildings you'll pass on your **way** _____ out of town are an **attorney's** _____ office and a **hockey** _____ rink. There will be signs for Route **Eight** _____ just past the rink. Make sure you head **east** _____.
- You'll probably see people **strolling** _____ past **Starlight** _____ Pond, about **thirteen** _____ miles outside of town.
- You'll pass several **golden** _____ **wheat** _____ **fields** _____ on your left. When you see an **old** _____ barn on your **right** _____, you're **almost** _____ there.
- Cross the **train** _____ tracks, turn down **Winding** _____ Way Lane, and look for the **yellow** _____ house. (There are only two houses on my **street** _____, so it shouldn't be hard to spot!)

NAME ___________________________

Lesson 1.12 Vowel Sounds (**oo**, **ew**, **ou**, **ui**)

- The letters **oo**, **ew**, **ou**, and **ui** can make the /oo/ sound, as in *l**oo**se*, *st**ew***, *y**ou**th*, and *br**ui**se*.
- The letters **oo** can also make the sound you hear in *wood*.

Read each clue. Fill in the letters to complete the word that matches the clue.

1. a piece of clothing worn for swimming — bathing s____ ____t
2. to take a short nap or sleep lightly — sn____ ____ze
3. appropriate — s____ ____table
4. the last car of a freight train — cab____ ____se
5. a place known for its movie stars — Hollyw____ ____d
6. a number of people gathered together — gr____ ____p
7. a problem or an annoyance — n____ ____sance
8. a type of nut — cash____ ____
9. a black-and-blue mark on the skin — br____ ____se

Read each sentence below. Complete the sentence by writing the word from the box that rhymes with the word in parentheses.

soup	new	tooth	neighborhood	scrapbook

1. The ________________ kids were invited to Bianca's eleventh birthday party. (understood)
2. Her favorite present was a ________________ from her best friend. (unhook)
3. Mrs. Delgado served bowls of spicy tortilla ________________. (group)
4. For dessert, there was a special *tres leches*, or three milks, cake to satisfy Bianca's sweet ________________. (booth)
5. After everyone had eaten, Bianca played a ________________ CD, so she and her friends could dance on the patio. (clue)

NAME ____________________

Lesson 1.12 Vowel Sounds (oo, ew, ou, ui)

Circle the letter of the word in each set that has the same vowel sound as the word in bold.

1. suitcase	**a.** exclude	**b.** shook	**c.** cluster
2. withdrew	**a.** merge	**b.** bamboo	**c.** mistook
3. crook	**a.** review	**b.** foot	**c.** blooming
4. through	**a.** brunch	**b.** rough	**c.** lagoon

Read the interview below. Circle the 18 words that have the same vowel sound as *boot* (spelled **oo**, **ew**, **ou**, or **ui**). Underline the five words that have the same vowel sound and spelling as *wood*. Do not circle the same word twice.

Cameron: I appreciate that you agreed to do this interview. I'm very interested to hear your point of view on your job and being an artist today.

Mr. Hopper: I'm happy to speak with you about my work. I think your interest in art is very cool.

C: What was your childhood like? When did you first know that you wanted to create cartoon characters?

MH: I always knew I wanted to be an artist. I wasn't sure what kind until I finished high school and a friend introduced me to some great cartoons.

C: How did you ever come up with a kangaroo who plays the kazoo or a tattooed baboon named Lou who dreams of traveling to the moon?

MH: I guess my characters seem pretty wacky. Ideas come easily to me, so I have to sift through them to find the ones that are suitable for a particular cartoon. Fatherhood has also been an inspiration. If I can create something my kids think is a hoot, there's a good chance other kids will like it too.

C: I'm so glad you took the time to talk with me. Any last words of advice?

MH: Art isn't an easy way to make your livelihood, but there is nothing that would be more satisfying for me. Best of luck in all your pursuits!

NAME ______________________________

Lesson 1.13 Vowel Sounds (**au**, **aw**, **al**, **all**)

- The vowel pairs **au** and **aw** can make the same sound, as in *c**au**ght* and ***aw**ful.*
- When the vowel **a** is followed by **l** or **ll**, as in *s**al**t* or *sm**all***, it makes the same sound as **au** and **aw** do.

Read the classified newspaper ads below. Underline the word from the pair in parentheses that has the same vowel sound as the word in bold.

- MISSING: **Small**, white dog with curly hair and fluffy tail. Answers to "Tucker." Please call 555-5486. Reward. (audio, calendar)

____

- **Sidewalk** sale at Clara's Closet, 615 E. Main St., June 11–14. Lots of great bargains on summer fashions. (trade, launch)

____

- HELP WANTED: Experienced mechanic to work mornings at Vinnie's **Auto** Repair. Call Vinnie at 555-1299 after 5:00. (malt, yarn)

____

- 2-bedroom vacation house in Poplar Beach available for the month of **August**. Five-minute walk to the beach. Call Rita at 555-6369. (crawl, hatch)

____

- Spaghetti and **meatball** supper at Glenview Road Senior Center. Saturday, June 11, 6:00 P.M. (prank, talking)

- Nature **walk** at Casson Falls Nature Preserve. Friday, June 10, 9:30 A.M. (salt, guard)

____

- **Author** Mai Ling signing children's books at Bay Ridge Library from 3:00–4:30 on Saturday, June 11. (branch, drawn)

____

- Vintage **pinball** machine for sale, circa 1984. Great condition—$250. Call Bryan at 555-6761. (daughter, enchant)

____

- Quality **lawn** care and maintenance by Delta Lawn Services. Mention this ad and get a 20% discount for the entire month of June! (faucet, fact)

____

- **Drawing** and painting classes available for kids ages 3–14. Visit www.bridgeportart.com for more information. (smart, birdcall)

NAME ______________________

Lesson 1.13 Vowel Sounds (**au**, **aw**, **al**, **all**)

Underline the word from the pair in parentheses that best completes each sentence below.

1. (Australia, August) is the sixth largest country in the world.
2. It is the world's (tallest, smallest) continent.
3. The indigenous, or native, people of Australia are often (talked, called) Aborigines.
4. The native people of Australia were treated (awfully, awkwardly) by people who arrived with hopes of settling and claiming the land.
5. (Recall, Because) Australia is fairly isolated, it has some interesting flora and (fauna, flaws) that are not found elsewhere in the world.
6. The koala seems like a sweet, cuddly creature, but it has very sharp (claws, stalks) that help it climb trees in the wild.
7. Australia is the driest inhabited continent, and the desert areas receive little (outlaw, rainfall).

Read each definition below. On the line, write the letter of the word that matches the definition.

1. ______ an American summer game	**a.** jigsaw
2. ______ what Jack climbed in the famous fairy tale	**b.** baseball
3. ______ a try-out for a play or other performance	**c.** coleslaw
4. ______ the season that follows summer	**d.** recall
5. ______ a popular type of puzzle	**e.** beanstalk
6. ______ to remember	**f.** autumn
7. ______ a side dish made with shredded cabbage	**g.** malt
8. ______ a sweet, cold drink, similar to a milkshake	**h.** audition

NAME ______________________

Lesson 1.14 Vowel Diphthongs

When two vowel sounds come together and create a new sound, the combination they form is called a **diphthong** (dip thong).
• The diphthong **oi**, as in *join*, and **oy**, as in *voyage*, make the same sound.

Read the paragraphs below. Underline the ten words that contain the /oi/ sound spelled **oi** or **oy**. You do not need to underline the same word more than once.

A boycott is a refusal to do business with a company that is believed to be doing something that is morally wrong. For example, the company may be known for exploiting its workers. The employees may not receive fair wages or good health care. Some protesters hope that by joining together they can shame a company into behaving better. Sometimes, the goal is to hurt the company financially so that it changes its ways.

Boycotts can be good for the public because they remind people that they have a voice. They can support or avoid companies based on how they do business. Many people believe that a company must earn its customers' loyalty and work hard not to disappoint them.

One of the most famous boycotts in history was the Montgomery bus boycott, which began in December of 1955 and lasted about a year. The point of the boycott was to protest the segregation of buses in Montgomery, Alabama. Rosa Parks, who refused to give up her seat on a bus, kicked off the boycott. A year later, the United States Supreme Court made segregated buses illegal and people everywhere rejoiced.

On the lines, list each underlined word from above below the correct heading.

/oy/ as in *destroy*	/oy/ as in *ointment*	
______	______	______
______	______	______
______	______	
	______	
	______	

NAME ___________________________

Lesson 1.14 Vowel Diphthongs

The diphthong **ou**, as in *blouse*, and **ow**, as in *scowl*, make the same sound.

Read the paragraphs below. Circle the six words that contain the /ow/ sound spelled **ow**. Underline the eight words that contain the /ow/ sound spelled **ou**. You do not need to underline the same word more than once.

The word *Chinatown* refers to a section of a city that has a large number of Chinese people and businesses even though the city itself is not Chinese. Today, Chinatowns can be found all around the world. In North America, many were formed in the 1800s when the Chinese faced much discrimination. Luckily, things are different nowadays, and Chinatowns are seen as interesting places to visit—full of local culture, foods, and other goods.

Chinatowns are often located in urban settings, near the downtown areas of large cities. A large red arch with Chinese characters often marks the entrance to Chinatown. In the past, the arches were gifts from China, but today many are built locally. Street signs in Chinatown are often bilingual, or written in more than one language. Most Chinatowns abound with restaurants. Some serve authentic Chinese dishes. Others are visited by tourists and serve dishes like chop suey or chow mein.

Since some business owners still have strong ties to China, there are many stores that sell Chinese goods. For example, they carry loud Chinese firecrackers for the New Year celebration and colorful paper lanterns. The markets sell large amounts of Asian foods that may be difficult to find elsewhere. In Chinatown, it is easy to pick up some seaweed, black duck eggs, oyster sauce, and countless types of fowl.

If you have the chance, it's worth taking the time to prowl the streets of a Chinatown near you. The sights and sounds are sure to astound you.

NAME ______________________________

Review Vowel Sounds and Diphthongs

- The letters **oo**, **ew**, **ou**, and **ui** can all make the /oo/ sound, as in *m**oo**se*, *kn**ew***, *s**ou**p*, and *cr**ui**se*. The letters **oo** can also make the sound you hear in wood.
- The letters **au** and **aw** can make the same sound as **a** does when it is followed by **l** or **ll**, as in ***au**thor*, *str**aw***, *s**al**t*, *over**all***.

Read each clue. Unscramble the letters beside it to find the word that matches the clue. Write the answers in the numbered spaces in the crossword puzzle.

Across

1. a place where people can walk beside the road (swiadlek)
3. Niagara Falls is a _____ (wlalftera)
6. a homophone for *through* (rewth)
7. a type of nut (wcsahe)
8. a mammal with a ringed tail (craoocn)

Down

1. a bag used for travel (ictseuas)
2. early morning, just as the sun is rising (wdna)
4. the part of a plant that grows underground (toor)
5. a sale in which people bid money for items (onatiuc)

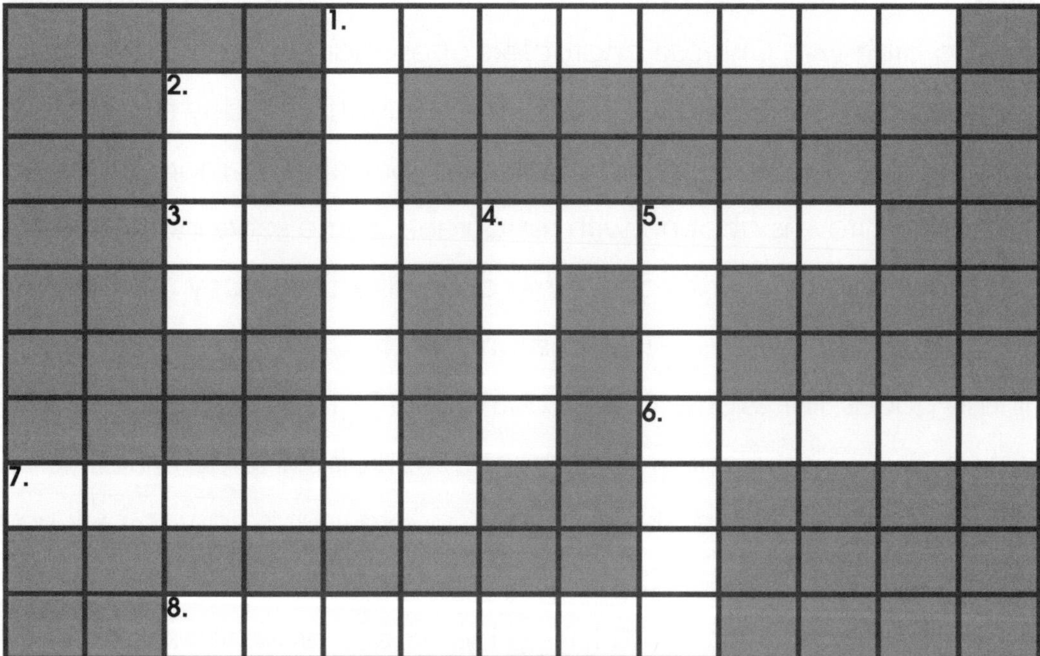

NAME ______________________________

Review Vowel Sounds and Diphthongs

- The diphthongs **oi** and **oy** can make the same sound, as in *bro**i**l, anno**y***.
- The diphthongs **ou** and **ow** can make the same sound, as in *am**ou**nt, cr**ow**n*.

Read each clue below. Fill in the blanks with the diphthong **oi**, **oy**, **ou**, or **ow** to form a word that matches the clue.

1. to wreck — destr_____ _____
2. to say something incorrectly — mispron_____ _____nce
3. a bright blue stone; also a color name — turqu_____ _____se
4. one of two thin strips of hair on the face — eyebr_____ _____
5. to rot or go bad — sp_____ _____l
6. an old-fashioned outdoor bathroom — outh_____ _____se
7. the capital of Russia — Mosc_____ _____

REVIEW: CHAPTER 1 LESSONS 12–14

Read the sentences below. On the line, write the word from the box that best completes each sentence and contains the diphthong listed in parentheses.

moist	noise	Scouts	sirloin	cookout	brownies
about	appointed	campground	without	boys	

1. The Boy __________________ (ou) arrived at the __________________ (ou) just before noon.
2. There was a great deal of __________________ (oi) and excitement as they explored the site.
3. The Scoutmaster __________________ (oi) one person in each tent to be in charge.
4. Somehow, the __________________ (oy) managed to set up their tents in __________________ (ou) 45 minutes __________________ (ou) too much trouble.
5. They were looking forward to an evening __________________ (ou) of ground __________________ (oi) burgers, corn on the cob, and __________________ (oi) chocolate __________________ (ow).

NAME ______________________

Lesson 1.15 The Schwa Sound

The **schwa sound** is the /uh/ sound you hear at the beginning of the word *around* and at the end of the word *pencil*. The vowels **a**, **e**, **i**, **o**, and **u** can all make the schwa sound, which is represented by this symbol: ə.

In each word below, the vowel that makes the schwa sound is set in bold.

about towe**l** lent**i**l pil**o**t cact**u**s

Read the sentences below. Circle the vowel that makes the schwa sound in each bold word.

1. Stella's older sister graduated from college as an English **major**.
2. Malik and his family visited Egypt and saw the **pyramids**.
3. Madeline always takes the **tomatoes** off her hamburgers.
4. Those chocolate-chip cookies were made from my grandmother's **recipe**.
5. The convenience store kept some of its soda cans in a **barrel** filled with ice.
6. A **severe** weather alert scrolled across the bottom of the TV screen.
7. I wasn't **aware** of how late I'd slept until I saw lunch on the table.
8. Chiara was surprised that the **dinosaur** skeleton wasn't very large.
9. We went to see the **pandas** at the National Zoo.

Read each set of words below. Underline the word that contains the /ə/ sound.

1. forget	breakdown	gather
2. willow	humor	soil
3. oxygen	movie	clubhouse
4. loyal	lonely	childhood
5. exciting	amount	smear
6. cruise	piano	coconut

NAME ______________________________

Lesson 1.15 The Schwa Sound

Read the paragraphs below. On the lines, rewrite the words that contain a schwa with their correct spellings.

Pluto, a dwarf planet in our solar systəm ________________, one day will have a visətər ________________. On January 19, 2006, NASA launched *New Horizons*, the first space probe heading to the outskirts of our solər ________________ system to study Pluto.

Norməlly ________________, the journey would take decades, but *New Horizons* was launched on an unusually powərfəl ________________ rocket. Shortly after liftoff, the spacecraft was hurtling əway ________________ from Earth at nearly 36,000 miles per hour! At that speed, *New Hərizəns* ________________ will reach Pluto in less than ten years.

The first stop, though, is Jupətər ________________. The probe will become the giənt ________________ planet's first visitor since Galileo stopped orbiting it in 2003.

By the summər ________________ of 2015, the spacecraft will be studying Pluto and sending photographs back to Earth. What will *New Horizons* discovər ________________ about this tiny, mysterious planet?

Look at each picture below. Write the word from the box that names the picture and the vowel that makes the schwa sound.

pencil	dragon	totem	pasta

____

____

____

____

____

____

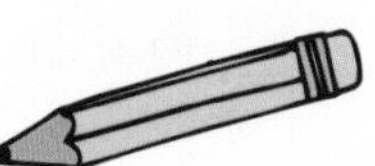

____

____

NAME ______________________________

Lesson 1.15 The Schwa Sound

Many words that end in a consonant plus **le** contain the schwa sound.

puzzle (puzzəl) buckle (buckəl) struggle (struggəl)

Read the story below. On the line, rewrite each bold word using the symbol for a schwa (ə) in place of the letters that make the schwa sound.

Once there were two poor peddlers who went from door to door, trying to **peddle** ____________________ their goods. The villagers **grumbled** ____________________ at the sight of the peddlers.

The poor peddlers built a small fire and balanced the empty pot on top. The older peddler put a small stone, not much bigger than a **pebble** ____________________, in the pot. He added a **drizzle** ____________________ of water and began to stir it.

"What's that?" asked a woman in a **purple** ____________________ scarf.

"Stone soup," replied the peddler. "If only we had a bit of cabbage."

"Cabbage?" cried a man. "I've a wee bit of cabbage to spare."

"Cabbage is splendid," said Jacob. "Too bad we don't have any potatoes."

"A potato's no **trouble** ____________________," said a tiny, **wrinkled** ____________________ woman with a **cackle** ____________________.

"I have a ham bone," said a young woman. "I was planning to let my **beagle** ____________________ **nibble** ____________________ on it."

And so it went. Before long, a delicious stew bubbled over the fire. When asked where they had found such a magical stone, the peddlers looked at each other with a **twinkle** ____________________ in their eyes. A magic stone, indeed, is hard to find.

NAME ______________________________

Lesson 1.15 The Schwa Sound

When a word is divided into syllables, one syllable is often said with more stress. The schwa sound is usually found in unstressed syllables.

Here are some words that have the schwa sound. The vowel that makes the sound is set in bold. Notice how the schwa sound appears in the unstressed syllable in each word.: **a**·lone′, ev′·i·d**e**nce, o′·d**o**r, s**u**·spense′.

Read the sentences below. For each bold word, underline the unstressed syllable and circle the vowel that makes the schwa sound.

1. Bernarr Macfadden was known as the "**Fa·ther** of Physical Culture."
2. In 1903, he founded the Coney Island **Po·lar** Bear Club.
3. **Mem·bers** of the club go swimming in the ocean during the **win·ter**.
4. Macfadden believed that the cold **wa·ter** was good for one's health.
5. The Coney **Is·land** Club isn't the only group of **ba·thers** who like the shock of taking a dip in frigid temperatures.
6. People all **a·round** the country share a passion for this unusual habit.
7. **To·day**, the members of the Coney Island Club swim every Sunday from October through **A·pril**.
8. Early in the **sea·son**, the temperature is in the low 60s, but later in the winter, it drops to **a·bout** 33 degrees.
9. The **swim·mers** wear nothing but regular bathing suits and surf boots to protect their feet.
10. On New Year's Day 2005, they raised money for the **Spe·cial** Olympics.
11. More than **se·ven** hundred swimmers headed for the icy Atlantic that day.
12. There is **e·ven** a movie about the Polar Bear Club and Coney Island in winter called *Side Shows by the Sea Shore*.

NAME ______________________

Lesson 1.16 The Sounds of **y**

- The letter **y** can make the /y/ sound you hear in ***y**esterday.*
- It can make the long **i** sound, as in *wh**y*** and *l**y**ing.*
- The letter **y** can make the long **e** sound at the end of a word, as in *twent**y***.
- In the middle of a word, **y** can make the short **i** sound, as in *g**y**mnast.*

Read the words in the box. Write each word below the correct heading.

celery	physical	python	yogurt	Egypt	yak
jellyfish	story	sky	analyze	yowling	typical

/y/, as in *yam*	long **i**, as in *try*	short **i**, as in *gym*	long **e**, as in *city*
________	________	________	________
________	________	________	________
________	________	________	________

Each of the following sentences contains a misspelled word. On the line, rewrite the word correctly by replacing one of the vowels with **y**.

1. When Miranda played soccer during gim, she scored a goal. ________
2. At the zoo, Brianna watched the hienas pacing inside their cage. ________
3. "Tommy, please come help me carre in the groceries!" ________
4. No one ever solved the mistery of the juice stain on the Harrises' living room rug. ________
5. Our English teacher said that not all poems rhime. ________
6. The recreation center had a huge suppli of games. ________
7. What is your favorite stile of music? ________
8. Most people think the Loch Ness monster is just a mith. ________

NAME ______________________

Lesson 1.16 The Sounds of y

Read the recipe below. List the bold words in the correct categories following the recipe. Hint: One word belongs in two categories.

- Most people think that making their own **yogurt** is a **very** complicated or **mysterious** process. It's **probably** much easier than **you** might imagine. All you need to begin is four cups of one-percent or two-percent milk and two tablespoons of plain, low-fat yogurt to get your batch started. (For extra **creamy** yogurt, use whole milk.)
- In a large pan, heat the milk over medium heat until it bubbles. Take it off the heat **immediately**, and measure the temperature with a cooking thermometer. It should read **approximately** 110°. Stir in the two tablespoons of yogurt, and put the mixture into a large glass container.
- **Tightly** cover it with a lid or some plastic wrap. Put it in the oven overnight with the oven light or pilot light on. To see if it has set, shake the container **gently**. If it isn't thick enough **yet**, put it back in the oven for a couple more hours. Once **your** yogurt is **finally ready**, keep it refrigerated.
- There are all sorts of **yummy** dishes you can make with homemade yogurt. **Try** a **typical** smoothie with some yogurt, blueberries, bananas, and **honey**. Chop up a **strawberry** or two, and serve it with granola. **Buy** some vegetables and make a dip with spices and seasonings. It's always good to keep a **supply** of yogurt on hand. And don't forget to save a couple of tablespoons as a starter for your next batch.

long **i** spelled **y**: ______________ ______________ ______________

long **e** spelled **y**: ______________ ______________ ______________

______________ ______________ ______________

______________ ______________ ______________

______________ ______________ ______________

short **i** spelled **y**: ______________ ______________

/y/ spelled **y**: ______________ ______________ ______________

______________ ______________

NAME ______________________________

Lesson 1.17 R-Controlled Vowels (**ar**, **er**, **ir**, **or**, **ur**)

When the letter **r** follows a vowel, it can change the vowel's sound.
- The letters **ar** make the sound you hear in *guit**ar***.
- The letters **or** make the sound you hear in ***tor**ch*.
- The letters **er**, **ir**, and **ur** can all make the same sound, as in *obs**er**ve*, *sk**ir**t*, and *ret**ur**n*.

Read each set of words below. Circle the word that has the same **r**-controlled vowel sound as the bold word.

1. **father**	person	smart	horde
2. **darkness**	careless	particular	scorch
3. **florist**	market	generous	border
4. **nocturnal**	birth	recording	harmful
5. **platform**	curtain	square	sworn
6. **regarding**	portion	version	farther
7. **whirl**	sports	harpoon	squirrel
8. **discard**	weather	exporting	alarm
9. **seashore**	support	argument	undershirt

Read each clue below. Unscramble the letters beside it to find the word that matches the clue. Each word will contain an **r**-controlled vowel.

1. to keep or protect from harm	**sepreerv**	______________
2. a person who protects swimmers	**eguldifar**	______________
3. to pay no attention to something	**egnior**	______________
4. annoy	**rbditus**	______________
5. a grassy area behind a house	**ckybraad**	______________
6. the nut of an oak tree	**oancr**	______________

NAME ____________________

Lesson 1.17 R-Controlled Vowels (**ar**, **er**, **ir**, **or**, **ur**)

Read the paragraphs below. Circle the 24 words that have the /ər/ sound, as in *paper* and *bird*. You do not need to mark the same word more than once.

Read the history of the American Revolution, and you will discover the name *Molly Pitcher*. Molly was not just one person, however. "Molly Pitcher" was the nickname given to many women who carried water to the thirsty soldiers. Despite their name, these women actually used buckets and not pitchers.

In the famous story about Molly Pitcher, Molly's husband operates a cannon. When he is injured, Molly bravely takes over his duties for the remainder of the battle. Later, George Washington honors Molly by making her an army officer. From then on, she is known as *Sergeant Molly*.

Something like this actually happened to at least two women. During the Battle of Monmouth in 1778, Mary Hays took over the cannon her injured husband had been firing, and she helped hold off the British. Many people consider Mary to have been the "real" Molly Pitcher.

Two years earlier, though, a battle raged on Manhattan Island in New York. When Margaret Corbin's husband, John, was killed in battle, she took over his cannon duties. Margaret fought hard until she was harmed by gunshot. After the war, Margaret worked with other injured veterans and became known as *Captain Molly*.

Through the years, these two stories merged together and became the story of Molly Pitcher as it is known today.

NAME ______________________

Lesson 1.18 More r-Controlled Vowels (air, are, ear, eer)

- The letters **air** and **are** can make the same sound, as in *despair* and *square*.
- The letters **ear** and **eer** can make the same sound, as in *spear* and *sneer*. The letters **ear** can also make the sound you hear in *wear*.

Read each clue below. Choose one of the **r**-controlled vowel combinations from the box to correctly complete the word that matches each clue.

ear	air	are	eer

1. the same job held for many years — car________
2. sloppy or reckless — c________less
3. a way to go from one floor to the next — st________s
4. came forth — app________ed
5. extra — sp________
6. directed a car or bicycle — st________ed
7. obviously — cl________ly
8. having on the body — w________ing
9. deep sadness — desp________
10. smudged or distorted — sm________ed

Read each set of words below. Underline the word that has a different **r**-controlled vowel sound than the rest of the words in the set.

1. snare	volunteer	bearing	unfair
2. nightmare	zero	peer	pioneer
3. hair	gear	square	underwear
4. spear	upstairs	fear	reindeer
5. millionaire	reappear	wheelchair	uncaring
6. impaired	prepared	seared	stare

NAME ______________________________

Lesson 1.18 More r-Controlled Vowels (air, are, ear, eer)

Read the paragraphs below. Underline the word from the pair in parentheses that has the same **r**-controlled vowel sound as the bold word beside it.

When he was only fifteen **years** (swear, spear) old, Rick Hansen was in a serious car accident that left him unable to walk. It took time for Rick to become accustomed to life in a **wheelchair** (welfare, pioneer). He never **despaired** (pear, bookmark), though, and he didn't let it change his dreams. He began training and won 19 international marathons. In 1984, he achieved one of his goals when he competed for Canada in the Olympic Games.

With all his accomplishments, Rick was just beginning to **prepare** (sharpen, affair) for his greatest challenge yet. He decided to wheel around the world to raise money and **awareness** (bear, appear) for people with disabilities. Rick **dared** (guard, pair) to think big, and it paid off. With help from some generous **volunteers** (reindeer, chairman), Rick traveled through rain and snow. He **steered** (sweep, sneer) over mountains and through deserts, **wearing** (rearview, swearing) out 160 wheelchair tires in the process.

The trip took Rick two years, two months, and two days. He journeyed more than 24,000 miles, through 34 countries on four continents. He raised the amazing sum of 26 million dollars during his Man in Motion World Tour. Without a doubt, Rick made it **clear** (underwear, steer) that almost anything can be achieved with hard work and a good attitude.

Today, the purpose of Rick's **career** (deer, share) is to improve the quality of life for people with spinal cord injuries. Rick has provided hope and inspiration for thousands of his **peers** (disappear, repair) who are disabled in some way.

Rick is certainly **aware** (square, gear) that life can be **unfair** (clearly, flare). But he has never let obstacles stand in his way or **impair** (jeer, stare) his ability to dream. If anything, challenges just make Rick work harder and **care** (airplane, carpet) more.

NAME ______________________

Review Schwa, the Sounds of y, and r-Controlled Vowels

- Remember, the schwa sound (ə) can be made by the letters **a**, **e**, **i**, **o**, or **u**. (**a**gree, tunn**e**l, Apr**i**l, gall**o**p, caref**u**l)
- It usually appears in unstressed syllables. (sis′·**te**r)
- It is often found in words that end in a consonant plus **le**. (dimple, dimpəl)

Read the words below. Circle the word in each set that contains the schwa sound. If you aren't sure, try saying the words out loud to yourself.

1. cruise	seven	rowboat
2. filthy	America	destroy
3. stumble	money	strength
4. quality	circus	olive
5. dismiss	sculptor	sardine
6. dignity	monkey	ruffle

Read each definition and the word beside it. On the line, rewrite the word with the correct vowel in place of the schwa.

1. not polite; rude — im′·pə·lite ______________

2. freedom or independence — lib′·ər·ty ______________

3. of or relating to Egypt — E·gyp′·tiən ______________

4. shaped like an egg — o′·vəl ______________

5. to greet — wel′·cəme ______________

6. a color of dark red — mə·roon′ ______________

7. to mutter or complain — grum′·bəl ______________

8. to love or worship — ə·dore′ ______________

9. an antonym for *close* — o′·pən ______________

10. a type of tree and a type of syrup — ma′·pəl ______________

NAME ______________________

Review Schwa, the Sounds of **y**, and **r**-Controlled Vowels

Read each sentence. Circle the word below the sentence that has the same sound of **y** as the bold word.

1. **Kyle** would rather be in the garden than just about anywhere else.

   nylon youth Egypt

2. His **yard** is filled with interesting and exotic plants.

   type yield geometry

3. On a **typical** summer day, Kyle might spend five or six hours outside.

   supply yellow system

4. His newest addition is a **yucca** plant, which he says has many edible parts.

   firefly yo-yo cheerfully

5. Kyle owns a **nursery** called the *Green Thumb*.

   suddenly yowling skylark

Circle each word that contains an **r**-controlled vowel in the proverbs below.

1. A picture is worth a thousand words.
2. One good turn deserves another.
3. Give and take is fair play.
4. Short visits make long friends.
5. A quitter never wins, and a winner never quits.
6. Leave no stone unturned.
7. Appearances can be deceptive.
8. The darkest hour is just before the dawn.
9. Great oaks from little acorns grow.
10. A bird in hand is worth two in the bush.
11. An apple a day keeps the doctor away.
12. Misery loves company.

NAME ____________________

Lesson 2.1 Base Words and Inflectional Endings

A **base word** is a word without endings added to it.
- Double the consonant before adding -**ed** or -**ing** to a base word with a short vowel sound that ends in a consonant. (shrug, shrugg**ed**, shrugg**ing**)
- If a base word ends with **e**, drop the **e** before adding the endings -**ed** or -**ing**. (skate, skat**ed**, skat**ing**)
- If a base word ends with **y**, change the **y** to **i** before adding the ending -**ed**. Do not change the **y** before adding the ending -**ing**. (marry, marr**ied**, marr**ying**)

Read the letter below. On the line, write the base word for each word in bold.

Dear Kylie,

I am so **excited** ____________ that we're going to be pen pals. I've been **reading** ____________ about New Zealand ever since I **discovered** ____________ that we were going to be **writing** ____________. I guess I'll start by **telling** ____________ you about myself.

I am ten years old and in the fifth grade. I like **living** ____________ in Chicago because there is so much to do. I have two brothers, 7 and 12, and a stepsister who is 18. Do you have any siblings? My mom and stepdad got **married** ____________ about four years ago. I **loved** ____________ finally **getting** ____________ a big sister. I'm **hoping** ____________ that she doesn't end up **choosing** ____________ a college that's too far from the Windy City.

I like **running** ____________, **listening** ____________ to music, and **dancing** ____________. What kind of music do you like? I'm so curious about life in New Zealand. Autumn is just **beginning** ____________ here. What season is it for you?

Your newest friend,

Lia

NAME ______________________

Lesson 2.1 Base Words and Inflectional Endings

Add the endings **-s** or **-es** to base words to form new words.

- Adding **s** to the end of some verbs changes their form.
  The monkeys leap. The monkey leap**s**.
- If a verb ends with **y**, change the **y** to **i** and add **es**.
  Noah and Mickey hurry. Noah hurr**ies**.
- If a verb ends with **s**, **sh**, **ch**, **x**, or **z**, add **es**.
  The officers search. The officer search**es**.

Read the paragraphs below. Underline the word from the pair in parentheses that correctly completes each sentence.

Every spring, the men and boys in my family (travel, travels) to a cabin about four hours away. Mom (call, calls) it our "Boys Getting Back to Nature" weekend. Everyone has a job while we're there. Uncle Lex (fetchs, fetches) the firewood. Grandpa Joe (supplys, supplies) us with all kinds of tasty baked goods, like muffins and thick, hearty loaves of bread. My oldest cousin, Will, (tosses, toss's) around a football with the younger cousins while Uncle Albert (catches, catchs) the fish we'll clean and grill for dinner.

Dad brings along his famous bullhorn, which (amplifys, amplifies) his voice so much, I'm sure that people miles away can hear it. He says it (keepes, keeps) anyone from wandering away from the group and getting lost. At night, the mosquitoes (buzzes, buzz) around us, but since we're covered in bug spray, they don't bite too much. Everyone (relaxes, relaxs) and (watchs, watches) the stars come out one by one. Grandpa tells his scariest story, which always (terrifies, terrifys) Danny, the youngest—or at least he (pretendes, pretends) it does. Thirty years from now, I hope I'll be sitting on that same porch with Dad's bullhorn and my own sons beside me.

NAME ______________________

Lesson 2.2 Comparative Endings

Comparative endings, such as -**er** and -**est**, are endings that change the meanings of base words.

- Add **er** to mean *more* when comparing two things. Add **est** to mean *most* when comparing three or more things.
  calm**er** = more calm   calm**est** = most calm
- For words that end in **e**, drop the **e** and add **er** or **est**. (wise, wis**er**, wis**est**)
- For words that end in a consonant plus **y**, change **y** to **i** before adding **er** or **est**. (crazy, craz**ier**, craz**iest**)
- For words that have a short vowel sound and end in a consonant, double the consonant before adding **er** or **est**. (slim, slimm**er**, slimm**est**)

Read the sentences below. On the line, write the base word for each bold word.

1. The **tallest** apartment building in the world is Trump World Towers in New York City. ______________
2. The **heaviest** freight train ever weighed 220 million pounds. ______________
3. Yellowstone National Park is **older** than Sequoia Park. ______________
4. The **biggest** Ferris wheel in the country is called the *Texas Star* and measures 212 feet. ______________
5. The **sunniest** place in the United States is Yuma, Arizona. ______________
6. The country of Luxembourg is **richer** than Norway. ______________
7. On average, it is **windier** in New Orleans than it is in Valdez, Alaska. ______________
8. The world's **smelliest** flower, the corpse flower, releases a terrible stench when it blooms. ______________
9. The Tacoma Narrows suspension bridge is **higher** than Japan's Akashi-Kaikyo suspension bridge. ______________

NAME ____________________

Lesson 2.2 Comparative Endings

Some comparisons are made by adding the word *more* or *most* in front of the adjective instead of adding an ending.

comfortable, **more** comfortable   fearful, **most** fearful

Underline the word or words in parentheses that correctly completes each sentence.

1. Adrian Millstone has been a zookeeper for 30 years, and he says that every year has been (interestinger, more interesting) than the last.
2. "What is the (most dangerous, dangerousest) animal you work with?" is the question Adrian is asked more often than any other.
3. People also ask him what the (rarest, rarer) animal at the zoo is.
4. The turtles' pool is (shallower, most shallow) than the alligators' pool.
5. Adrian keeps the lights (more dim, dimmer) in the aquarium than in the other buildings.
6. The (unusualest, most unusual) animal Adrian has cared for is a cave-dwelling lizard that has no eyes but has an amazing sense of smell.

On the lines below, write two comparative sentences using the words in the box. You do not need to use all the words.

big	wise	friendly	warm	strange	dangerous	wet

1. ____________________

____

2. ____________________

____

Phonics Connection

Circle the words from the Word Box that contain the soft **g** sound. Underline the words that contain the hard **g** sound.

NAME ______________________________

Review Base Words, Inflectional Endings, and Comparative Endings

Read each word below. On the line, write the base word.

1. crunches ____________________
2. prepares ____________________
3. buries ____________________
4. polishes ____________________
5. regrets ____________________
6. perceives ____________________
7. coaxes ____________________
8. petrifies ____________________
9. denies ____________________
10. reduces ____________________
11. scurries ____________________
12. laughs ____________________

Read the sentences below. Add **s** or **es** to each base word in parentheses to complete the sentence. Remember that you may need to change the spelling of the word before adding the ending.

1. Antonio (dream) ____________________ the same dream over and over again.
2. He (guess) ____________________ that he has dreamed this dream at least 30 times.
3. He (stand) ____________________ in a stadium as a crowd of fans (cry) ____________________ his name.
4. The high ceiling (amplify) ____________________ their voices.
5. He (hurry) ____________________ across the court to the sound of chanting and (search) ____________________ for the faces of his parents in the stands.
6. The ref (toss) ____________________ him the ball, and he can feel its bumpy skin in his hand.
7. The ball (beat) ____________________ a fast, regular rhythm on the court, and Antonio (relax) ____________________ slightly for just a moment.
8. He (try) ____________________ to focus as the ball (leave) ____________________ his hands and (soar) ____________________ toward the basket.
9. The buzzer (buzz) ____________________ and Antonio (wake) ____________________ up without ever knowing if he made the basket.

NAME ______________________

Review Base Words, Inflectional Endings, and Comparative Endings

Solve each problem below. Be sure to remember the rules for adding endings. On the second line, write a sentence using your answer.

1. escape + ed = ______________

   ____

2. grin + ing = ______________

   ____

3. empty + ing = ______________

   ____

4. freeze + ing = ______________

   ____

5. worry + ed = ______________

   ____

Fill in the blanks below with the correct forms of the comparative words.

Base Word	"More"	"Most"
______________	______________	most careful
______________	stickier	______________
close	______________	______________
______________	thinner	______________
sleepy	______________	______________
______________	more popular	______________
sad	______________	______________
______________	______________	earliest
valuable	______________	______________
______________	______________	safest

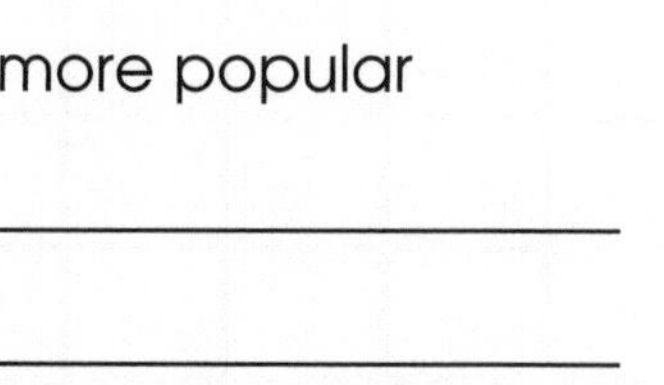

NAME ____________________

Lesson 2.3 Plurals

Most plurals are formed by adding **s** to the end of a word. (turtle, turtle**s**)

- If a noun ends in **sh**, **ch**, **s**, or **x**, add **es**. — couch, couch**es**
- If a noun ends with a consonant + **y**, drop the **y** and add **ies**. — party, part**ies**
- Form the plural of most words that end in **f** by just adding **s**. For some words that end in **f** or **fe**, change the **f** or **fe** to **v** and add **es**. — roof, roof**s**; loaf, loa**ves**

Read each clue. Unscramble the letters beside it to find the plural form of the word that matches the clue and write it on the line. Then, find each word in the word search puzzle.

1. a small mammal with red fur and pointy ears (xefos) ____________________
2. a long piece of clothing that keeps the neck warm (esarcvs) ____________________
3. a frozen treat that comes on a stick (lesposipc) ____________________
4. a public place that lends books to people (elsaribri) ____________________
5. two pieces of bread with meat or cheese filling (chsdwiaens) ____________________
6. the hard covering on the feet of animals like deer (vshooe) ____________________
7. a book in which one writes private thoughts (ardeiis) ____________________

h	p	g	t	j	i	q	m	v	h	o	o	v	e	s
f	o	x	e	s	s	s	k	l	q	k	p	b	v	c
r	p	g	u	w	v	s	o	p	n	e	b	e	r	a
h	s	a	n	d	w	i	c	h	e	s	r	t	t	r
d	i	a	r	i	e	s	g	h	a	n	m	e	o	v
h	c	y	w	j	n	c	j	a	u	i	r	p	g	e
j	l	i	b	r	a	r	i	e	s	t	y	g	b	s
h	e	j	p	e	e	s	s	b	n	d	r	l	t	m
h	s	r	b	d	j	u	h	p	o	r	v	e	s	r

NAME ______________________

Lesson 2.3 Plurals

- Form the plural of words that end with a vowel + **o**, by adding **s**.
  radio, radio**s** trio, trio**s**
- Form the plural of words that end with a consonant + **o**, by adding **es**.
  volcano, volcano**es** echo, echo**es**
- The following words do not follow this pattern: *photo, burro, auto, Eskimo, pro, piano, solo, soprano, rhino, burrito, sombrero, pueblo,* and *dynamo*. Just add **s** to make their plural forms.

Read each clue below. Choose the word from the box that matches the clue and write its plural form on the line.

flamingo	pistachio	mango	potato	rodeo

1. a rounded white tuber often cooked as a vegetable ______________
2. a sweet tropical fruit that has bright yellow flesh ______________
3. a pale-green edible nut; often used to flavor ice cream ______________
4. a sport that includes bull riding and calf roping ______________
5. a tall, bright pink bird that often stands on one foot ______________

Read the following newspaper headlines. On each line, write the plural form of the word in parentheses.

1. Father and Son (Hero) ______________ Save Family from Burning Building
2. Three Female (Kangaroo) ______________ on Loan from Sydney Zoo
3. Manufacturer Recalls (Shampoo) ______________ for Causing Skin Rashes
4. Local Farmer Breeds Two New Strains of (Tomato) ______________

Phonics Connection

Which two plural words in exercise 2 have the same vowel sound as *stew*?

______________ ______________

NAME ____________________

Lesson 2.4 Irregular Plurals

Some words have **irregular plural forms.**

child, children　　foot, feet　　die, dice　　goose, geese　　ox, oxen

woman, women　　man, men　　mouse, mice　　tooth, teeth

The singular and plural forms of the following words are the same: *deer, fish, moose, sheep, trout, salmon, wheat, series, traffic,* and *species.*

Fill in the blanks in each item below.

1. an ox	a herd of __________
2. a single __________	a flock of sheep
3. the __________	11 moose
4. one __________	a gaggle of geese
5. one salmon	three __________
6. the deer	a family of __________

Use the pictures to help you fill in the blanks in the problems below.

1. four - one mouse = __________

2. one die + two = __________

3. five teeth - one = __________

4. three  + one  = __________

5. two 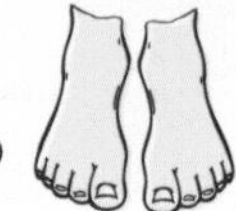 + two 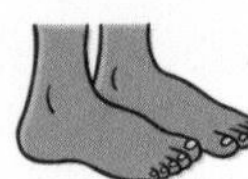 = __________

NAME ______________________

Lesson 2.4 Irregular Plurals

Read the sentences below. Use the words in parentheses to fill in each blank with the word that best completes the sentence.

1. There will be eight ________________ in the play, but Bradley is the youngest ________________ to have a speaking part. (child, children)
2. Grandpa has been feeding all the ________________ at Mill Pond for more than 20 years, but his favorite is a fat, ornery ________________ named *Bert*. (goose, geese)
3. Rachel feeds ________________ to her pet snake, Oliver. Yesterday, one ________________ escaped from Oliver's cage. (mouse, mice)
4. Anya hurt her left ________________ when she slipped on the snow that Ivan had tracked inside on his ________________. (foot, feet)
5. Don't worry if you can't find the ________________ that rolled under the couch. There are a couple of extra ________________ in the box. (die, dice)
6. Gavin chipped one ________________ playing hockey, but the rest of his ________________ seem to be in good shape. (tooth, teeth)

Read the sentences below. If the bold word is spelled correctly, make a check mark on the line. If it is not, write the correct spelling on the line.

1. ________________ How many **serieses** of books has Daniel Pinkwater written?
2. ________________ Please wash the sand off your **feets** before you come inside.
3. ________________ Jessy chose six new **fish** for her tank.
4. ________________ Do you think the **women** will score enough points to win?

Phonics Connection

Write the four words in parentheses from above that have the long **i** sound.

________________ ________________ ________________ ________________

NAME ______________________

Lesson 2.5 Possessives

Form a **possessive**, or word that shows ownership, by adding an apostrophe (') and an **s** to the end of a word. Treat words that end in **s** the same way.

Riley'**s** trumpet   Chris'**s** friends

To form a **plural possessive**, add an apostrophe to the end of a plural word.

the cats**'** tails   the girls**'** laughter

If a plural word does not end in **s**, add an apostrophe plus **s**.

the people**'s** cars   the children**'s** books

Read the paragraphs below. If the word in bold is plural, write **PL** on the line. If it is singular possessive, write **SP**. If it is plural possessive, write **PP**.

In 2004, Sandra Day O'Connor came in sixth on a list of the **World's** ______ Most Powerful Women. How did **Texas's** ______ favorite cowgirl become so famous and respected? O'Connor served as the first female associate justice of the Supreme Court. She was nominated in 1981 during Ronald **Reagan's** ______ presidency. As the only woman serving on the Supreme Court, the **country's** ______ attention was often focused on O'Connor. She received more than 60,000 **letters** ______ from people during her first year on the job! This surprised her, and she was glad when Ruth Bader **Ginsburg's** ______ arrival in 1993 focused **people's** ______ attention elsewhere.

During O'Connor's nearly 25 **years** ______ on the bench, she played a major role in many important court **decisions** ______. The **justice's** ______ reputation as being politically moderate, or in the middle, meant that her vote was extra important. She was often a swing vote, or deciding vote, on **cases** ______ that got a lot of attention.

NAME ______________________________

Lesson 2.5 Possessives

Read each sentence below. Circle the possessives and underline the objects of the possessives.

1. Winnie Foster is the main character in Natalie Babbit's book *Tuck Everlasting*.
2. The book *Cowboys and Longhorns* tells about the cowboys' struggle to run longhorn cattle from Texas to Kansas.
3. There are many amazing photographs in the nonfiction book *Volcanoes: Journey to the Crater's Edge*.
4. *The Watsons Go to Birmingham—1963* by Christopher Paul Curtis tells about the Watsons' experiences as they travel south one summer.
5. In *Holes* by Louis Sachar, Stanley Yelnats figures out how to change his family's bad luck.
6. *Millicent Min, Girl Genius* is about an 11-year-old girl's life and how she copes with the challenges of growing up.
7. Kevin Henkes's book *Olive's Ocean* was published in 2003.
8. Gary Paulsen has written four books about the same character, but I like *Brian's Winter* best.
9. *There's a Boy in the Girls' Bathroom* is my favorite Louis Sachar novel.
10. Karen Cushman has written several historical novels, like *The Midwife's Apprentice*.
11. Ruby Bridges's story of integrating an all-white elementary school in 1960 is told in *Through My Eyes*.
12. *The Penderwicks: A Summer Tale of Four Sisters, Two Rabbits, and a Very Interesting Boy* won the National Book Award for Young People's Literature.
13. In *Esperanza Rising*, Esperanza's life changes when she must move to California and live at a migrant farm workers' camp.

NAME ______________________________

Review Plurals, Irregular Plurals, and Possessives

Underline the correct form of each word in parentheses.

1. A group of (geese, gooses) is called a *gaggle* or a *flock*.
2. A group of (buffalos, buffaloes) is called a *herd*.
3. A group of (lions, lions') is called a *pride*.
4. A group of (finches, finchs) is called a *charm*.
5. A group of (mosquitos, mosquitoes) is called a *swarm*.
6. A group of (wolfs, wolves) is called a *pack* or a *route*.
7. A group of (oxen, oxes) is called a *yoke*, a *drove*, a *team*, or a *herd*.
8. A group of (fox, foxes) is called a *skulk* or a *leash*.
9. A group of (rhinoes, rhinos) is called a *crash* or a *herd*.
10. A group of (trout, trouts) is called a *hover*.

Fill in the blanks to complete the chart below.

Singular	Plural	Singular Possessive	Plural Possessive
		pastry's	
auto			
	grasses		
		enemy's	
	mice		
portfolio			
		branch's	

Phonics Connection

1. Which word in exercise 1 begins with a silent consonant pair? ____________________
2. Find two words in exercise 1 in which **s** makes different sounds. Write the words on the lines. ____________________ ____________________

NAME ______________________

Review Plurals, Irregular Plurals, and Possessives

Read the letter below. Find the seven possessives and circle them. On the lines following the paragraphs, rewrite the possessives you circled.

Ex.: the boys' hockey sticks   the hockey sticks belonging to the boys

Dear Victoria,

Thanks for your last letter. How's school going? I just started taking violin lessons a few weeks ago. My sister's violin had been sitting in the closet for years, and my parents decided someone needed to use it. I love playing the violin. My teacher's name is Louisa Valentino, and her son, Eddy, is in my class at school. My class's first recital is coming up on November 30.

I spent last weekend at the Watts' house. Erin's bedroom has a leaky ceiling, so we got to sleep in the basement while it was being fixed. The doors' hinges are squeaky since the house is so old, and Adam spent all night trying to scare us. We also watched a couple of movies. The movies' plots were so interesting that we totally lost track of time. We stayed up till 12 A.M. on Saturday!

Your cousin,

Kimberly Wi

1. ______________________
2. ______________________
3. ______________________
4. ______________________
5. ______________________
6. ______________________
7. ______________________

NAME ______________________________

Lesson 2.6 Compound Words

A **compound word** is a combination of two shorter words.

door + bell = doorbell   book + mark = bookmark

In **open compounds**, there is a space between the two words, but they refer to a single thing.   ice skate   fire drill   living room

Read each clue below. On the line, write the compound word that matches the clue. Draw a slash (/) to separate the two words within each compound word. Hint: One word is an open compound.

1. a trap used to catch a mouse ______________
2. the bud of a rose ______________
3. a storm during which there is thunder ______________
4. a machine used for mowing the lawn ______________
5. Grades 9–12 ______________
6. sauce made from mashed apples ______________

Read the words in both boxes below. On the lines that follow, combine the words to make as many compound words as possible.

Box A (first half of compound)

every	hand	down	sea	rain

Box B (second half of compound)

body	book	shore	shake	shell
where	made	coat	one	
hill	bow	town	food	stand
stairs	drop	thing	weed	

____

____

Phonics Connection

Which two words in the first exercise have the vowel sound you hear in *ball*? Circle the vowel pairs that make the sound.

______________   ______________

NAME ____________________

Lesson 2.6 Compound Words

Read the paragraphs below. Circle the 26 compound words. You do not need to circle the same word more than once. Hint: One is an open compound.

My favorite memories of childhood are visiting my grandparents at their home in Traverse City, Michigan. My parents would drop me off for the weekend, and I would bound up the stairs to greet Nonnie and Pop who were waiting outside on the doorstep. Pop would always give me a firm handshake that turned into a giant hug. Nonnie would take off her eyeglasses, give me a kiss, and hustle me into the kitchen so she could feed me.

Pop was a fantastic woodworker. He made my grandparents' dining room table, the dressers in all the bedrooms, and dozens of birdhouses. I loved how everything at Nonnie and Pop's house was handmade with love and care. Life at my house, with seven siblings, was hectic and chaotic. I liked the time alone with my grandparents. I liked poring over Nonnie's cookbooks for the perfect fudge recipe. Best of all, I liked helping Nonnie take care of the bees.

My grandmother's beehives were kept at the far edge of the yard. She had learned the art of beekeeping from her father, who used to sell his honey at roadside stands and local markets. According to Nonnie, her father was a wonderful storyteller. His customers would come for the honey and stay for the stories. Without a doubt, Nonnie inherited both talents from her father.

On summer nights, I'd sit on the porch with Nonnie and Pop, watch the sunset, and eat hot, buttery popcorn. She'd tell us stories about snowstorms in July, or a notebook full of secrets that her youngest brother had stolen and then shared with his entire classroom. There was something perfect and magical about those days with Nonnie and Pop. I think of them as I tend to the bees in my own garden, polish a bookcase my grandfather made, and tell stories of their lifetime and my own.

NAME ______________________________

Lesson 2.7 Contractions

- A **contraction** is an abbreviated, or short way, of writing two words. An apostrophe (') takes the place of the missing letters in a contraction.
  you're = you are we'll = we will here's = here is
- The words *will* and *not* form the contraction *won't.*

Fill in the blanks to complete the chart below.

Word +	Word =	Contraction
would		would've
they	will	
		aren't
I	have	
let		let's
there	would	
		he's
does	not	
we		we're

The following sentences contain incorrect contractions. On the line, rewrite each contraction correctly.

1. My mom does'nt know how to swim, but I've been taking lessons since I was little. ______________

2. Next year, I'll be able to join the intermediate swim team if theres an opening. ______________

3. My swimming instructor's name is Julie. If I were to make the team, she'ld be my coach, too. ______________

NAME ______________________________

Lesson 2.7 Contractions

Circle the 15 contractions in the passage below. Write the two words that make up each contraction on the lines that follow.

If you've ever thought about visiting a different country, you'll also want to know something about its customs and manners. If you aren't careful, a common American gesture might offend your hosts.

JAPAN

- Slurp while you eat your noodles. It'd be rude not to because slurping shows that the meal's delicious.
- Use your fingers carefully. Pointing isn't nice in Japan.

EGYPT

- Sit next to an Egyptian with your legs crossed and he'll probably move away. Showing him the soles of your feet is very offensive.

INDIA

- The left hand mustn't ever touch food.
- You shouldn't say thank you. That'll only insult your hosts.

RUSSIA

- You might've thought that standing with your hands in your pockets was okay, but in Russian, it's frowned upon.

TAIWAN

- In case you hadn't heard, touching someone's shoulder or head is rude.
- Don't wink at the locals. They'd be offended.

______________ ______________ ______________ ______________

______________ ______________ ______________ ______________

______________ ______________ ______________ ______________

______________ ______________ ______________

NAME ______________________

Review Compound Words and Contractions

Form a common compound word by drawing a line to match each word in column 1 to a word in column 2. Write the compound word on the line.

1. milk	storm	______________
2. sail	day	______________
3. motor	ball	______________
4. thunder	shake	______________
5. foot	quake	______________
6. wash	boat	______________
7. earth	cloth	______________
8. birth	cycle	______________

Use the pictures to help you fill in the blanks in the problems below.

1. 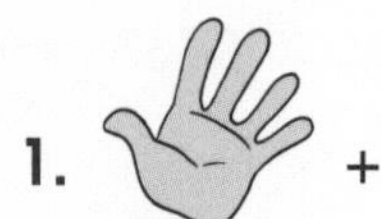 +  = ______________

2. + dust = ______________

3.  +  = ______________

4. +  = ______________

5.  + 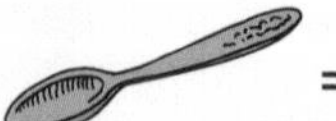 = ______________

6.  + back = ______________

Phonics Connection

Underline each word in the first exercise that contains an **r**-controlled vowel.

NAME ______________________

Review Compound Words and Contractions

Read the sentences below. On the line, write the contraction that the bold words would form if they were combined.

1. Although Romare Bearden is best remembered for his artwork, it **was not** ________________ his only talent or interest.

2. There are many career paths he **might have** ________________ chosen.

3. If you **have not** ________________ seen any of his work, **you will** ________________ be surprised at the variety of styles.

4. Bearden joined the Harlem Artists' Guild. **That is** ________________ where he was exposed to the work of masters like Picasso and Matisse.

5. During the Civil Rights movement, Bearden began working in collage—a medium for which **he would** ________________ become famous.

6. He also worked a good deal in photomontage. **It is** ________________ a form of art in which photos are cut up and joined together in different ways.

7. By looking at Bearden's paintings and collages, it is easy to see where **he has** ________________ lived and the things **that have** ________________ been important to him.

8. **There is** ________________ much to be learned about life and the African-American experience by taking the time to look carefully at Bearden's work.

9. If **you are** ________________ interested in learning more about Bearden and his art, visit your local library.

Phonics Connection

In the first exercise, find the following:

- a word in which **y** makes the long **i** sound ________________
- a word in which **y** makes the long **e** sound ________________
- a word in which **y** makes the /y/ sound ________________

NAME ______________________

Lesson 2.8 Prefixes

Adding a **prefix** to the beginning of a base word can change its meaning.
• The prefixes **un-**, **non-**, and **dis-** can mean *not* or *opposite of.*
unnatural = not natural **non**realistic = not realistic
disconnect = not connected

Read each clue below. Underline the word in parentheses that matches the clue. On the line, write the base word. If you need help, use a dictionary.

1. not seen (nonseen, unseen) ______________
2. not equal (unequal, disequal) ______________
3. not specific (nonspecific, disspecific) ______________
4. not familiar (disfamiliar, unfamiliar) ______________
5. not athletic (nonathletic, disathletic) ______________

Read the paragraphs below. Circle the 11 words that have prefixes.

I put on my first pair of ice skates when I was six. I couldn't believe how uncomfortable they were. My feet were unsteady, and I could barely stand. My teacher, Gail, asked the class to skate to her at the other side of the rink. We all just stood there and stared at her uncertainly. No one wanted to disobey the teacher, but we were unsure how to get from one side of the rink to the other. Finally, I got down on my hands and knees and crawled across the ice to my teacher. Gail laughed in disbelief as the entire class followed.

You might think that I would have been disqualified or unwelcome in the skating world forever, but Gail liked my creative thinking. For the last six years, she's helped me train nonstop for this competition. I've felt uneasy for months, but now I'm ready to put on my skates and have some fun. I know I won't be disappointed. I'm ready to win.

NAME ___________________________

Lesson 2.8 Prefixes

- The prefix **co**- means *together*. **co**pilot = to pilot together
- The prefix **mid**- means *middle*. **mid**afternoon = middle of the afternoon
- The prefixes **in**- and **im**- mean *not*.
  improper = not proper **in**direct = not direct

Read the clues below. Choose the word from the box that matches each clue, and write it in the numbered space in the crossword puzzle.

coworkers	immature	coexisting	impractical	midterm	coeducation	incorrect

Across

3. existing together
4. middle of the term
6. not practical
7. not correct

Down

1. people who work together
2. educating together
5. not mature

NAME ______________________

Lesson 2.8 Prefixes

- The prefix **pre**- means *before*. — **pre**test = test before
- The prefix **post**- means *after* or *later*. — **post**test = to test after
- The prefix **re**- means *again*. — **re**learn = learn again
- The prefix **mis**- means *wrongly* or *badly*. — **mis**judge = judge wrongly

Replace each set of bold words in the sentences with a word from the box.

postelection	rechecked	restate	preview	misread
misheard	preordered	retraced	misunderstood	

1. The **after the election** ________________ party was held at Anna's apartment.

2. Anna had **ordered before** ________________ plenty of food for the guests.

3. Unfortunately, the candidate had **understood wrongly** ________________ the directions that Anna had given him.

4. He **checked again** ________________ his notes before he called the apartment.

5. "I must have **heard wrongly** ________________ the name of your street," he said.

6. "What does your apartment building look like?" asked the candidate as he **traced again** ________________ his steps down the street.

7. Suddenly, he heard Anna gasp. "It looks like they **wrongly read** ________________ the results. You're leading the race by 11 percent of the votes!"

8. A few minutes later, the candidate stood before his supporters. "I cannot **state again** ________________ often enough how important you all were in this election."

9. "It was just a **before view** ________________ of what's to come. Imagine all we can accomplish this year!"

NAME ____________________

Lesson 2.8 Prefixes

- The prefix **uni**- means *one*. — **uni**color = one color
- The prefix **bi**- means *two*. — **bi**monthly = every two months
- The prefix **tri**- means *three*. — **tri**angle = having three angles
- The prefix **multi**- means *many*. — **multi**level = having many levels

Read the sentences below. Underline the word from the pair in parentheses that best completes each sentence.

1. How will we raise enough money for brand-new softball (uniforms, triforms)?
2. Mr. Fox is (bilingual, trilingual). He speaks Russian, Greek, and Japanese.
3. Every morning, Pedro takes a (multivitamin, univitamin) with his breakfast.
4. *The Golden Compass*, *The Subtle Knife*, and *The Amber Spyglass* are the books in a (trilogy, biology) written by Philip Pullman.
5. A dinosaur called (biceratops, triceratops) had two large horns on its head and a third smaller horn on its nose.
6. Rye Hill Elementary is hosting (Multicultural, Unicultural) Awareness Day so that students can learn about many different cultures and lifestyles.
7. Dad's new (multifocals, bifocals) allow him to see things clearly close-up and at a distance.
8. America's (unicolor, tricolor) flag is a symbol of freedom to many people.
9. There were celebrations all around the country during America's (bicentennial, multicentennial) in 1976.
10. The (bistate, tristate) area, which includes Ohio, Kentucky, and Indiana, was hit with a blizzard that left as much as 16 inches of snow in some places.
11. The (tricycle, unicycle) is similar to a bicycle, except that it has only one wheel and requires a very good sense of balance.

NAME ____________________

Lesson 2.8 Prefixes

- The prefix **over**- means *too much.*
  overcook = cook too much
- The prefix **under**- means *too little* or *below.*
  underground = below ground
- The prefix **sub**- means *under, less than,* or *below.*
  substandard = below the standard
- The prefix **super**- means *above, extra,* or *greater than.*
  supersoft = extra soft

Read the clues below. Each answer will contain the prefix **over**- or **under**-. Write your answer on the line.

1. An antonym for *underuse* is ____________________.
2. An antonym for *overdone* is ____________________.
3. An antonym for *overcharge* is ____________________.
4. An antonym for *undersized* is ____________________.
5. An antonym for *overcook* is ____________________.

Read each sentence below. On the line, write a word from the box to take the place of the bold words.

subzero	superabsorbent	supersensitive	subaquatic	superfine

1. The **extra fine** sand sticks to my arms and legs, so Mom has to hose me off before I come in the house. ____________________
2. The temperature for Saturday's game will be **below zero**. ____________________
3. The paper towel ad claims this brand is **extra absorbent**. ____________________
4. The marine biologist is interested in **below the water** life. ____________________
5. Celine is **extra sensitive** to animal fur and dander. ____________________

NAME ______________________________

Lesson 2.8 Prefixes

- The prefix **en**- means *in*, *into*, or *make*. **en**sure = make sure
- The prefix **anti**- means *against*. **anti**war = against war
- The prefix **semi**- means *half* or *partly*. **semi**finished = half finished

Read the words and the clues below. Circle the prefixes in the words in the second column. On the line, write the letter of the word that matches each clue.

1. ______ somewhat formal	**a.** antibacterial
2. ______ partly conscious	**b.** anticrime
3. ______ against bacteria	**c.** semicircle
4. ______ in trust	**d.** entangle
5. ______ half a circle	**e.** semiformal
6. ______ to make tangled	**f.** entrust
7. ______ against crime	**g.** semiconscious

Underline the word from the pair in parentheses that best completes each sentence.

1. Cameron got dressed in the (semiweekly, semidarkness) of early morning.
2. He slapped together a sandwich and grabbed an apple and some oatmeal cookies that were speckled with (semisweet, semisolid) chocolate chips.
3. Cameron twisted the doorknob on his way out, (ensuring, enabling) that it was locked behind him.
4. As he stepped outside, he was (enforced, engulfed) by the smells wafting from the *panadería*, or Spanish bakery, a few blocks away.
5. Cameron removed the special (antifreeze, antitheft) lock from his bike and wheeled it onto the sidewalk.
6. As he sped down the quiet street in the cool morning air, he was glad that Mr. Capitano had (encouraged, enfolded) him to take the paper delivery job.

NAME ______________________

Lesson 2.9 Suffixes

Adding a **suffix** to the end of a base word can change its meaning.

The suffixes -**ion**, -**sion**, and -**tion** all mean the *act of*, *state of*, or *quality of*.
- suspen**sion** = the act of suspending registra**tion** = the act of registering

Read the paragraph below. Circle the 11 words that end with the suffix -**ion**, -**sion**, or -**tion**.

A Norwegian man named Kjell Sandved has a rather unusual passion. He photographs things in nature that look like letters or numbers. He first made the decision to pursue this project when he saw the letter **F** on the wing of a butterfly. Sandved started seeing letters and numbers everywhere he looked in nature. A coiled snake looked like the letter **Q.** A spider wove a perfect **X** of silk through the center of its web. Even before he started taking photos, Sandved had a great appreciation for the environment. His fascination grew as he saw more and more images. The completion of Sandved's project took a great deal of devotion and determination—as well as more than 20 years and visits to 30 different countries.

Are the letters and numbers some form of communication for plants and animals? Not really. The identification of these shapes and forms is just something the human eye is used to searching for. The patterns may hold some attraction for other animals of the same species. They might also frighten off predators or help an animal blend into its surroundings.

What is Sandved's next mission? He is currently looking for designs in nature that look like eyes, faces, and other shapes, like cats and mice.

Choose four words you circled and write their meanings on the lines below.

______________ ______________________________

______________ ______________________________

______________ ______________________________

______________ ______________________________

NAME ______________________

Lesson 2.9 Suffixes

- The suffixes -**able** and -**ible** both mean *can be* or *able to be*.
  crush**able** = able to be crushed collect**ible** = can be collected
- The suffixes -**ty** and -**ity** mean *state of* or *condition of*.
  special**ty** = condition of being special

Read the clues and the words beside them. Circle the correctly spelled word that matches each clue.

1. the condition of being safe	safeable	safety	safeity
2. able to be exchanged	exchangeable	exchangeible	exchangity
3. the condition of being generous	generosty	generousness	generosity
4. the state of being humid	humidable	humidty	humidity
5. can be allowed	allowable	allowible	allowing

Read the sentences below. Choose the word or words from the box that best complete each sentence and write them on the lines.

memorable	irresistible	impossible	loyalty	honesty	ability

1. Arriving on time will be ________________ because of the traffic jam.

2. Mira's best qualities are ________________, ________________, and a good sense of humor.

3. The day my brother was born was the most ________________ day of my life.

4. The smells coming from the bakery were almost ________________.

5. Jack inherited his ________________ to sing from his grandpa.

Phonics Connection

1. Which word in the box above contains a vowel diphthong? ________________

2. Which two words in the second exercise contain the same long **o** spelling as *hostess*?

____

____

NAME ______________________

Lesson 2.9 Suffixes

- The suffix -**en** means *made of* or *to make*. short**en** = to make short

For words that have a short vowel sound and end in a consonant, double the consonant before adding **en**.

mad → mad**den** = to make mad

- The suffix -**ic** means *like* or *having the character of*. hero**ic** = like a hero

Read the clues below. Add a suffix to each word in bold to correctly match the clue, and write the new word on the line. Hint: You must change the spellings of some words before you can add a suffix.

1. have **sympathy** ______________
2. make **sharp** ______________
3. having the character a **romance** ______________
4. have **enthusiasm** ______________
5. make **lighter** ______________
6. make **deeper** ______________
7. have **optimism** ______________

Read the sentences below. Underline the correct word from the pair in parentheses to complete each sentence.

1. A huge (wovic, woven) rug covered the Thompsons' living room floor.
2. On our history test, we were expected to know the (specific, specifen) dates of (historen, historic) events.
3. Be sure you (straighten, straightic) the house before our guests arrive.
4. When I play chess, I try to take a (strategic, strategen) approach.
5. Orange barrels lined our block because the city was getting ready to (broadic, broaden) the road.

NAME ______________________

Lesson 2.9 Suffixes

- The suffixes -**ness** and -**ship** both mean *state of being* or *condition of.*
  kind**ness** = state of being kind owner**ship** = state of being an owner
- The suffixes -**ance** and -**ence** mean *state of being* or *the act of.*
  resist**ance** = the act of resisting prefer**ence** = the act of preferring

Read the paragraphs below. Circle each word that ends with **ness**, **ship**, **ance** or **ence**. Choose four of these words and define them on the lines that follow.

Almost every American today has an awareness of Paul Revere's midnight ride, but few know that he had some assistance in becoming famous.

By trade, Revere was a silversmith who was known for his fine craftsmanship. During the Revolutionary War, he and William Dawes were asked to warn Samuel Adams and John Hancock that the British were coming to arrest them. Later, a third man, Samuel Prescott, joined them. On the way to Lexington, Revere alerted sleeping townspeople to the circumstances. He is said to have rode through the darkness shouting his warning.

The men were captured by British troops, but Dawes and Prescott escaped. Later that evening, Revere was released without his horse. There's no doubt that the bravery, persistence, and quickness of these men helped the Americans defend themselves against the enemy and win their independence.

It wasn't until Henry Wadsworth Longfellow wrote his famous poem, "Paul Revere's Ride," that Revere's performance became so well known. But Longfellow was a writer, not a historian. He had a fondness for good stories, including those that weren't precisely true. Even though the endurance and the hardships of three men contributed to the victory, Paul Revere is the only one recognized in the poem.

______________ ______________________________

______________ ______________________________

______________ ______________________________

______________ ______________________________

NAME ______________________________

Lesson 2.9 Suffixes

- The suffix -**ish** means *like, about,* or *somewhat.*
  baby**ish** = like a baby
- The suffix -**ist** means *one who makes or practices.*
  violin**ist** = one who plays the violin

Read the sentences below. Add **ish** or **ist** to each word in parentheses to correctly complete the sentence. Remember, you may need to change the spelling of the base word before you add the suffix.

1. On stormy days, the lake's water has a ____________________ tint. (green)
2. My cousin is the lead ____________________ in a reggae band. (guitar)
3. The play takes place in England, so I have to speak with a ____________________ accent. (Britain)
4. A safety ____________________ addressed the students after the fire drill. (special)
5. Assuming you know what a person is like based on his or her skin color is ____________________. (race)
6. The pop singer bounded onstage dressed in ____________________ clothing. (style)

Read the following job descriptions. Using the word in bold as a clue, write the correct name of the career being described.

1. someone who works in a **pharmacy**: ____________________
2. someone who creates **art**: ____________________
3. someone who does **dental** work: ____________________
4. someone who writes **novels**: ____________________
5. someone who studies **geology**, or the science of Earth: ____________________
6. someone who sells and arranges **flowers**: ____________________

NAME ____________________

Lesson 2.9 Suffixes

Some words have more than one suffix.

help**fully** (-**ful**, -**ly**) child**ishness** (-**ish**, -**ness**)
reason**ably** (-**able**, -**ly**) inspira**tional** (-**tion**, -**al**)

Circle the word or words that contain more than one suffix in each advertisement below. Make a slash (/) between the two suffixes.

There's a cure for your out-of-control thirstiness. Try **Cool Blast Sports** drink today! Available in six cool flavors.

Orchard Patch apple drink, which is naturally and artificially flavored, contains **nine** vitamins and minerals.

Cranberries are traditionally used at Thanksgiving, but they can be a colorful, healthy part of your everyday diet.

Smile Bright toothpaste is historically proven to give you **whiter teeth** and the smile you dream of.

IS GREATER FLEXIBILITY YOUR GOAL? TRY NEW **LIFT 'N' STRETCH WEIGHTS!**

Send RubyBelle and Co. greeting cards, and your friends and family will never forget your thoughtfulness.

On the lines below, write two ads of your own. You can use words from the box, or you can think of other words that contain more than one suffix.

truthfulness	decoratively	skillfulness	gradually

1. ____________________

2. ____________________

Phonics Connection

1. What sound does **y** make in the words in the box above? ____________

2. On the lines, write two words in which **y** makes a different sound.

____________ ____________

NAME ___________________________

Review Prefixes and Suffixes

Use the table to help you remember the meanings of the prefixes you learned.

un-, **non-**, **dis-**, **in-**, **im-** = not			**mis-** = wrongly or badly
re- = again			**anti-** = against
pre- = before			**post-** = after, later
super- = above, extra			**sub-** = under or less than
over- = too much, above			**under-** = too little, below
co- = together			**mid-** = middle
en- = in, into, or make			**semi-** = half, partly
uni- = one	**bi-** = two	**tri-** = three	**multi-** = many

The survey below was made by the Ridgemore Environmental Task Force (RETF) to understand people's views on the environment. Replace each set of bold words with a word from the box.

biweekly	reuse	inexpensive	recycle	antipollution	ensure	overcrowded	unable

- How much of your trash do you **cycle again** ____________________?
- If you are **not able** ____________________ to recycle something, do you ever try to **use** it **again** ____________________?
- Would you be willing to purchase a **not expensive** ____________________ bin for storing newspapers?
- Do you have any ideas about how we can **make sure** ____________________ that all residents of Ridgemore know what recycling services are offered?
- Do you feel that our roads have become **too crowded** ____________________?
- Would you be able to attend the **every other week** ____________________ meetings to become a member of the task force?
- Are you willing to campaign for the new **against pollution** ____________________ laws?

NAME ___________________________

Review Prefixes and Suffixes

Use the table to help you remember the meanings of the suffixes you learned.

-ion, **-sion**, **-tion** = act, state, or quality of	**-able**, **-ible** = can be or able to be
-ty, **-ity** = state of or condition of	**-en** = made of or to make
-ic = having the character of	**-ness**, **-ship** = state of being
-ance, **-ence** = state of being or the act of	**-ish** = like, about, or somewhat
-ist = one who makes or practices	

Read the clues below. Find the word in the box that matches each clue and write it on the line.

happiness violinist citizenship noticeable reversible generosity straighten enthusiastic congratulation magnetic fragrance biologist foolish intelligence

1. the state of being fragrant ______________
2. like a fool ______________
3. able to be noticed ______________
4. to make straight ______________
5. the state of being happy ______________
6. having the character of enthusiasm ______________
7. condition of being generous ______________
8. act of congratulating ______________
9. one who practices or studies biology ______________
10. able to be reversed ______________
11. state of being a citizen ______________
12. one who plays the violin ______________
13. having the character of a magnet ______________
14. the state of being intelligent ______________

NAME ____________________

Lesson 2.10 Syllables

Words can be divided into parts called **syllables**. Each syllable has one vowel sound. The number of vowel sounds equals the number of syllables.

desk = 1 vowel sound = 1 syllable
ques·tion = 2 vowel sounds = 2 syllables
how·ev·er = 3 vowel sounds = 3 syllables
reg·u·lar·ly = 4 vowel sounds = 4 syllables

Look at each picture below. Choose the word from the box that names the picture and write it on the first line. On the second line, write the number of vowel sounds you hear when you say the word out loud.

boots	pumpkin	umbrella	tornado	pretzel	caterpillar

____________________ ____________________

____________________ ____________________

____________________ ____________________

____________________ ____________________

____________________ ____________________

____________________ ____________________

Phonics Connection

Three words in the box contain the schwa sound. Rewrite them using the schwa symbol.

____________________ ____________________ ____________________

NAME ______________________________

Lesson 2.10 Syllables

- Compound words can be divided into syllables between the two parts of the compound.
  bath·robe light·house
- A word that has two consonants between two vowels (VCCV) is divided between consonants.
  den·tist cor·ner
- A word that has a prefix or suffix is divided between the prefix or suffix and the base word.
  re·place bright·ness
- If a word has the VCV pattern, listen to the first vowel sound. If it is long, the word is usually divided after the first vowel.
  a·corn **lo**·cust
- If it is short, the word is usually divided after the consonant.
  lev·el **pun**·ish

Draw slashes (/) through each bold word below to divide it into syllables.

The Westminster **Kennel** Club Dog Show is probably the best-known dog show in the country. People **travel** from all around to attend the **yearly** event at New York's Madison Square **Garden**. It first began in 1877 as a show **mostly** for **sporting** dogs. **Today**, it focuses more on the dogs' appearance rather than their **talents** or qualities as **working** animals.

Professional handlers show most dogs. The handlers know how to **showcase** the best qualities of each animal. **Winners** from each breed **compete** for the **title** "Best in Group." Some of the groups are working dogs, **herding** dogs, hound dogs, and sporting dogs. These **canines** then compete for the important title "Best in Show."

Over the years, many different breeds of dogs—from **sheepdogs** to Afghans to **bulldogs**—have won the popular title. Terriers, though, are a clear favorite. They have won **almost** half the Best in Show titles since 1907 when the **honor** was first given.

The winners **rarely** compete and win again. In fact, only six winners have **ever** had a **second** victory. Usually, they retire and earn a great deal of **money** by **breeding future** generations of champions.

NAME ______________________________

Review Syllables

Read the paragraphs below. On each line, write the number of vowel sounds you hear in the bold word beside it.

Toothbrushes and **toothpaste** ______ are **probably** ______ **things** ______ that you take for granted. An **ancient** ______ toothbrush might not have looked like the **colorful** ______ **plastic** ______ brush you're used to. The ancient **Egyptians** ______ and **Romans** ______ both used **something** ______ called a chew stick. It was made from a **twig** ______ that was **frayed** ______ on one end.

The first "**modern**" ______ toothbrush was **invented** ______ in **China** ______ in 1498. The **bristles** ______ were made of **coarse** ______ hair from **animals** ______ like pigs and horses. These modern toothbrushes didn't **really** ______ seem to catch on in **Europe** ______, though. An English **prisoner** ______ named William Addis is the **person** ______ who deserves credit for **devising** ______ the style of toothbrush that became **popular** ______ around the **world** ______. He made his first toothbrush by **gluing** ______ bristles from a **hairbrush** ______ into **holes** ______ he made in a small piece of bone.

Once **people** ______ began using Addis's toothbrushes, there was a **demand** ______ for some kind of tooth cleaning **powder** ______ or **paste** ______. The Egyptians had used a mixture of **vinegar** ______ and a crumbled **volcanic** ______ stone. It's hard to believe, but the Romans used urine because it contains natural **whitening** ______ elements. The more modern toothpastes used baking **soda** ______ as the main **ingredient** ______.

Try going to a large **drugstore** ______ today and counting how many **different** ______ kinds of brushes and pastes you can buy. There are dozens of **flavors** ______ of toothpaste. Do you think William Addis could have imagined an **electric** ______ toothbrush and **bubblegum** ______ flavored paste?

NAME ______________________

Review Syllables

Read the words in bold below. Draw slashes to divide each word into syllables. Then, circle the word beside it that has the same number of syllables.

1. **footstep**	fantastic	pepperoni	service
2. **club**	mitten	birds	bathrobe
3. **invention**	thunder	welcome	magical
4. **watermelon**	excuse	adorable	vacation
5. **bookcase**	refrigerate	sighed	effort

Underline each two-syllable word in the sentences below. Circle the three-syllable words. Then, draw a slash to divide the words into syllables.

1. Coretta Scott King was known as the wife of Martin Luther King but also as a civil rights activist herself.
2. She met her husband at the New England Conservatory.
3. Coretta's Freedom Concerts used both poetry and music to communicate with people and bring their attention to the issues she cared about.
4. Coretta opposed the Vietnam War and organized people in protest.
5. After her husband's death in 1968, Coretta worked to keep his memory and his dreams of peace and racial equality alive.
6. Coretta also worked to end racial segregation in South Africa.
7. The Coretta Scott King Book Award is given to outstanding African-American authors and illustrators of children's books.

Phonics Connection

Use the words in the first exercise to answer the questions below.

1. Write the two words in which **ti** makes the /sh/ sound. ______________

   ____
2. Which word contains a silent consonant pair? ______________

REVIEW: CHAPTER 2 LESSON 10

NAME ______________________

Lesson 3.1 Synonyms and Antonyms

- **Synonyms** are words that have the same or almost the same meanings.
  raise, increase   pick, choose   brave, courageous
- An **antonym** is a word that means the opposite of another word.
  ending, beginning   deep, shallow   boring, exciting

On the line, write the letter of the word that is a synonym for the bold word.

1. ______ **mistake**   **a.** error   **b.** remedy   **c.** solution
2. ______ **calm**   **a.** agitated   **b.** serene   **c.** asleep
3. ______ **bulge**   **a.** valley   **b.** swell   **c.** portion
4. ______ **peak**   **a.** bottom   **b.** level   **c.** summit
5. ______ **move**   **a.** transport   **b.** bury   **c.** return

Circle the word that is an antonym for each bold word below.

1. The word *peacock* is **accurate** only for males. Females are *peahens.*
   perhaps   inaccurate   ignorant
2. Several varieties of peafowl exist and are **native** to India, Java, and Africa.
   foreign   local   unusual
3. The green peafowl is in **danger** of extinction.
   excitement   loneliness   safety
4. The peacock's tailfeathers are its most **spectacular** feature.
   dull   beautiful   hidden
5. In comparison, the **female's** tailfeathers are shorter and duller in color.
   fowl's   bird's   male's
6. The purpose of the male's bright plumage is to **attract** a mate.
   repel   forget   frighten
7. The peacock's mating call sounds **similar** to a very loud cat's meow.
   somewhat   different   replaces

NAME ____________________

Lesson 3.1 Synonyms and Antonyms

Read each pair of words below. If the words are synonyms, write **S** on the line. If they are antonyms, write **A** on the line.

1. ______ break shatter
2. ______ generous stingy
3. ______ continue interrupt
4. ______ mend repair
5. ______ thaw melt
6. ______ arrive depart
7. ______ late tardy
8. ______ thin slender

Read each sentence below. On the line that follows, write a new sentence using an antonym for the bold word.

1. Key West, Florida, is located 90 miles **north** of Havana, Cuba.

   ____

2. There is a **sunset** celebration every evening at Mallory Square in Key West.

   ____

3. Key West is known for being home to many **unusual** or eccentric people, including writers, artists, musicians, and street performers.

   ____

4. The classic American writer Ernest Hemingway was not **born** in Key West but lived there for many years.

   ____

5. Today, you can visit his home and meet the descendants of his **famous** six-toed cats.

   ____

6. Shel Silverstein, author of *Where the Sidewalk Ends*, *A Light in the **Attic***, and *The Giving Tree*, lived and died in Key West.

   ____

7. The weather in Key West tends to be **mild**, similar to the Caribbean Islands.

   ____

NAME ______________________________

Lesson 3.1 Synonyms and Antonyms

Read the paragraphs below. If the word in bold is followed by an **A**, find an antonym from the box and write it on the line. If it is followed by an **S**, find a synonym and write it on the line.

smallest	occupations	problem	private	destroy	imaginative	few
assist	supply	while	unemployed	ended	totally	useless

The Works Projects Administration (WPA) was a program begun **during** (S) ____________________ Franklin D. Roosevelt's presidency. **Many** (A) ____________________ Americans were unemployed during the Great Depression. The government's **solution** (A) ____________________ was to **create** (A) ____________________ the WPA to **provide** (S) ____________________ **jobs** (S) ____________________. The WPA was **begun** (A) ____________________ in May of 1935. During the eight years that the WPA existed, 650,000 miles of roads, 78,000 bridges, and 125,000 **public** (A) ____________________ buildings were built.

The WPA also provided jobs for people in **creative** (S) ____________________ fields. Money was given to support actors, writers, and musicians. In fact, it was the **largest** (A) ____________________ amount of money ever given by the government to support the arts.

The WPA ended in 1943 when more work became available because of World War II. At that time, nine million people had been **employed** (A) ____________________ by the WPA. It didn't **completely** (S) ____________________ end the unemployment that the Depression created. Still, it did manage to **help** (S) ____________________ people hold on to their self-respect and create **useful** (A) ____________________ things.

NAME ______________________________

Lesson 3.1 Synonyms and Antonyms

Read the clues below. Find the word in the box that matches each clue, and write it on the line. Then, circle each word in the word search puzzle.

together	annoy	cautious	liberty	reply
straight	appear	present	consume	locate

1. an antonym for *alone* ____________________
2. a synonym for *freedom* ____________________
3. a synonym for *eat* ____________________
4. a synonym for *careful* ____________________
5. an antonym for *crooked* ____________________
6. a synonym for *find* ____________________
7. an antonym for *vanish* ____________________
8. an antonym for *absent* ____________________
9. a synonym for *bother* ____________________
10. a synonym for *respond* ____________________

t	c	u	p	e	g	g	y	t	e	b	s	l	k	f
h	a	p	p	e	a	r	n	l	o	c	a	t	e	n
j	u	h	y	y	w	n	a	i	h	o	p	h	v	s
f	t	b	p	s	g	m	u	b	q	n	g	d	z	n
o	i	o	r	r	w	f	q	e	h	s	v	q	f	l
t	o	g	e	t	h	e	r	r	d	u	e	p	m	r
v	u	c	s	j	u	f	k	t	a	m	z	k	g	e
r	s	a	e	t	t	p	b	y	n	e	o	p	e	p
r	a	n	n	o	y	e	a	v	b	f	l	p	r	l
g	t	c	t	u	b	h	a	d	s	l	j	u	i	y
k	t	a	y	e	x	s	t	r	a	i	g	h	t	n

NAME ______________________

Lesson 3.2 Shades of Meaning

You have already learned that synonyms are words that have the same or nearly the same meanings. When the meanings are not exactly the same, you have to think carefully about which word fits best in a sentence.

Because the words *quiz* and *test* have different shades of meaning, one word (*test*) better fits the sentence below.

The coach ran a *quiz* to check the chemicals in the school pool.

The coach ran a *test* to check the chemicals in the school pool.

One word in each sentence below does not fit. Find the word and cross it out. On the line, write the word from the box that better completes the sentence.

melted	bad	caught	grew	close

1. The oak tree developed more than 40 feet tall. ____________
2. The tomatoes we bought last week are already naughty. ____________
3. Jonathan forgot to seal the door when he left the house. ____________
4. I left a candy bar in the car, and it thawed all over the seat. ____________
5. The batter hit a pop fly, and Julio ensnared it in his glove. ____________

Read the sentences below. Underline the word from the pair in parentheses that best completes the sentence. On the line, write a sentence correctly using the word you did not underline.

1. Barney's glass of milk was too close to the (border, edge) of the table.

   ____

2. The runner stopped to drink some water and (relax, rest) for a moment.

   ____

3. The market was filled with a variety of (new, fresh) produce.

   ____

NAME ______________________________

Lesson 3.2 Shades of Meaning

Read the paragraphs below. Next to each bold word, write the word from the box that has a similar meaning but better completes the sentence.

machines	allowed	survives	tiny	returned	active
habitat	total	surface	creatures	lies	

Davidson Seamount, about 75 miles off the coast of Monterey Bay, California, is an underwater volcano that hasn't been **functioning** ________________ for millions of years. It is nearly 8,000 feet tall, yet its peak **reclines** ________________ about 4,000 feet underwater. Scientists mapped the seamount as early as the 1930s. It is only recent technology that has **authorized** ________________ them to begin really exploring the area deep below the **top** ________________.

This underwater **neighborhood** ________________ is home to all sorts of interesting marine life. Imagine "bubblegum" coral twice your height, fields of bright yellow sponges, purple sea fans, and clams with nearly transparent shells. These **beings** ________________, and many others, live in **entire** ________________ darkness in their own strange and fascinating world.

In 2006, researchers **backtracked** ________________ to Davidson Seamount to learn more about the coral forests growing there. The scientists used robotic **appliances** ________________, called *ROVs*, to explore, collect samples, and send back images to their computers. They wanted to learn more about how the coral **remains** ________________ at such great depths.

Wouldn't it be terrible if one day there really were no more mysteries to explore on Earth? Because scientists have discovered only a **microscopic** ________________ fraction of what Davidson Seamount has to offer, it doesn't look like that will happen anytime soon.

NAME ____________________

Lesson 3.3 Levels of Specificity

Some words give the reader more information than others.

- A general word, like *insect*, does not give the reader much information. A more specific word, like *beetle*, gives the reader an added detail. The word *ladybug* is more specific than both *insect* and *beetle*.

Read each clue and the set of words that follow it. Choose the word that is most specific and circle it.

1. I am a sweet chocolate treat. I can be made from a mix or from scratch.

   food brownie dessert

2. I have 88 black and white keys. I can make beautiful music.

   piano keyboard instrument

3. If you are good at working with numbers and symbols, you might enjoy me.

   math algebra subject

4. I am a very intense and unpleasant feeling.

   anger emotion rage

5. I am something you wear on your feet, especially when playing sports.

   clothing sneakers shoes

Draw a line to match each word in the column on the left with a more specific word from the list beside it.

1. game	sculptor
2. royalty	frog
3. language	dictionary
4. amphibian	Spanish
5. artist	king
6. book	checkers
7. building	Mars
8. school	kitchen
9. silverware	barn
10. organ	heart
11. planet	spoon
12. room	university

NAME ______________________

Lesson 3.3 Levels of Specificity

Read the sentences below. For each word in bold, there is a more specific word in the box. Find the word and write it on the line.

boats	Iguanodon	brother	lemonade	broccoli
evergreens	blizzard	watercolor	basketball	

1. For dinner, Dad and Sam are making pork chops, wild rice, and a **vegetable**. ______________
2. Three days a week, Izumi has **sport** practice after school. ______________
3. The Conroy twins plan to set up a **beverage** stand in their driveway this weekend. ______________
4. An enormous **storm** traveled across New England today, knocking out power and making the roads dangerous. ______________
5. I was amazed that we were allowed to touch an actual **dinosaur** bone at the museum. ______________
6. Xavier's oldest **sibling** just joined the Peace Corps and will spend the next two years in South America. ______________
7. The drawbridge slowly lifted so that the waiting **vehicles** could pass beneath it. ______________
8. Annabelle and her mom chose three different kinds of **trees** to plant in the backyard. ______________
9. My favorite piece of artwork from Ms. LaFaye's class is a small **painting** I did of the view from my bedroom window. ______________

Phonics Connection

Use the words in bold above to answer the question below.

Which two words contain consonant digraphs?

______________ ______________

NAME ____________________

Review Synonyms, Antonyms, Shades of Meaning, and Levels of Specificity

Read the paragraphs below and complete the activity that follows.

Petroglyphs are images carved into rock, usually by ancient peoples. Experts estimate that the oldest petroglyphs may be 12,000 years old. It is obvious that these carvings were some sort of communication, but no one is entirely sure of their exact purpose. Some may have had religious or cultural meanings, while others might have marked the boundaries between tribes. Some of the images, like humans, animals, and elements of nature, are easy to recognize. Others are still a mystery to the people who study them.

Petroglyphs have been found in all parts of the world, except for Antarctica. Scientists have noticed something interesting: the petroglyphs in different continents are sometimes very similar to one another. There is no way to know exactly why this is, but scientists do have several theories. People from one region of the world could have migrated to other regions and influenced the style of petroglyphs there. Some experts believe that the resemblance has to do with the way the human brain is wired and functions. Perhaps it is just a coincidence that the styles resemble one another.

1. In paragraph 1, find a synonym for *pictures*. ____________________
2. In paragraph 1, find an antonym for *difficult*. ____________________
3. In paragraph 1, find a synonym for *examine*. ____________________
4. In paragraph 1, find an antonym for *modern*. ____________________
5. In paragraph 1, find a synonym for *professionals*. ____________________
6. In paragraph 2, find a synonym for *affected*. ____________________
7. In paragraph 2, find a synonym for *area*. ____________________
8. In paragraph 2, find a synonym for *discovered*. ____________________
9. In paragraph 2, find an antonym for *ignored*. ____________________
10. In paragraph 2, find an antonym for *boring*. ____________________

NAME ______________________

Review Synonyms, Antonyms, Shades of Meaning, and Levels of Specificity

Read each pair of sentences below. Find the pair of words in the box that will complete the sentences. Write them on the lines, making sure that each word fits the meaning of the sentence.

vacant, empty	discovered, detected	help, aid	cure, heal

1. The archaeologists ________________ a complete dinosaur skeleton.

   The fire alarm ________________ smoke before anyone could smell it.

2. We called the hotel to see if they had any ________________ rooms.

   The refrigerator is nearly ________________, so we need to go to the store.

3. How long will it take for this wound to ________________?

   The doctor hopes to ________________ most of the patients with antibiotics.

4. The government came to the ________________ of its citizens when the storm struck.

   I think I'm going to need some ________________ studying for this test.

Read the sentences below. On the line, write the word from the box that best completes each sentence.

birthday	fossil	soprano	German	finger	symbol	loneliness	fabric	plaid

1. ________________ is a specific nationality.
2. ________________ is a specific pattern, which is a type of design.
3. A ________________ is a type of singer, who is a type of entertainer.
4. Silk is a specific type of ________________.
5. A ________________ is a specific type of rock.
6. A more general word for *letter* is ________________.
7. ________________ is a specific emotion.
8. A specific type of celebration is a ________________.
9. A pinky is a specific ________________, which is a specific digit.

REVIEW: CHAPTER 3 LESSONS 1–3

NAME ______________________________

Lesson 3.4 Homophones

Words that sound the same but have different spellings and meanings are called **homophones**.

Dad *brews* a fresh pot of coffee several times each day.

Francisco has a nasty *bruise* on his leg from playing soccer.

Read the menu below. Underline the word from the pair in parentheses that correctly completes each sentence or phrase.

(ANT, AUNT) ELLA'S DINER

Pancakes **$3.95**

(Eight, Ate) silver-dollar pancakes served with (reel, real) maple syrup and (you're, your) choice of (meat, meet).

Your choice of four breakfast (serials, cereals), served with milk or soy milk and fresh fruit. **$2.25**

Waffles **$3.95**

(Plane, Plain) or topped with blueberry sauce.

(Chews, Choose) your style of eggs: scrambled, fried, poached, or sunny-side-up. **$3.50**

LUNCH SPECIALS

Homemade (Chili, Chilly)

Served spicy or mild, with cornbread and cheese. Cup **$2.50**

Bowl **$4.00**

Chicken Soup **$4.95**

Comforting soup with chicken, celery, (carats, carrots), and (hour, our) special blend of herbs.

Drinks $1.00 Sun-(brewed, brood) iced-tea, pop, coffee, hot (tee, tea), and OJ.

* Ask about our homemade (deserts, desserts). They are (maid, made) fresh daily, and each (piece, peace) is large enough for (to, two) people to share.

NAME ____________________

Lesson 3.4 Homophones

Read the pairs of clues below. On the line, write each homophone from the box next to its definition.

stare, stair	night, knight	heard, herd	son, sun	heal, heel
sale, sail	lessen, lesson	meddle, medal	fair, fare	

1. to interfere ____________ an award ____________

2. a soldier of the Middle Ages ____________ evening ____________

3. a very hot ball of gases in the sky ____________ a male child ____________

4. to travel on a boat or ship ____________ to sell things at a reduced price ____________

5. a step ____________ to look intensely at something ____________

6. honest or just ____________ money paid to travel by bus or plane ____________

7. something that is taught ____________ to make less ____________

8. to make better ____________ the back of the foot ____________

9. a group of animals, like deer ____________ the past tense of *hear* ____________

NAME ___________________________

Lesson 3.5 Multiple-Meaning Words

A word that has more than one meaning is called a **multiple-meaning word**, or **homograph**. The context of a sentence can help you determine which meaning the author intends.

The *batter* hit the ball, and the crowd watched it soar over the fence.

The *batter* sizzled as Dad closed the lid to the waffle maker.

Read each sentence below. On the line, write a sentence using another meaning of the bold word. If you need help, you may use a dictionary.

1. Dozens of creatures lived in the grasses growing along the **bank** of the river.

____

2. The small brown rabbits **bound** away when they hear humans approaching.

____

3. A young **buck** with a small rack of antlers stops to drink from the stream.

____

4. The young **swallow** eagerly demand its breakfast.

____

5. It is **rare** to see raccoons here in the middle of the day.

____

6. After a while, the bear cubs **tire** of chasing one another through the field.

____

Phonics Connection

1. Which word in the first sentence contains an **r**-controlled vowel?

____

2. Which word in the second sentence contains an **r**-controlled vowel?

____

NAME ____________________

Lesson 3.5 Multiple-Meaning Words

Read the paragraphs and the pairs of definitions below. On the line following each bold word, write the letter of the definition as it is used in the passage.

Charley rode his **moped** ______ up the Wilson's driveway. He barely had enough room to **park** ______, because a boat took up most of the space. Mr. Wilson was putting fishing poles into a **hatch** ______ in the boat's deck. Charley gave Mr. Wilson a quick **wave** ______ as he approached the boat.

Charley peered inside and saw a layer of dust covering every **surface** ______. Mr. Wilson would be cleaning all morning.

When Charley asked if Sean was home, Mr. Wilson replied that Sean and his mom had gone to buy **produce** ______. "They should be back soon," he added.

Mr. Wilson pulled out a tangled mess of ropes **wound** ______ around each other and asked Charley to help him sort it out. When the ropes were separated, Mr. Wilson had Charley **wind** ______ them into neat coils.

"As soon as the boat's ready, Charley, you'll join Sean and me on our first fishing trip. Hopefully, we'll catch some huge **bass** ______!"

moped:
a. acted sad
b. a motorized bike

park:
a. stop a vehicle
b. a place for recreation

hatch:
a. a small door or opening
b. to emerge from an egg

wave:
a. moving water
b. a hand gesture

surface:
a. come up
b. outer or top layer

produce:
a. fruits and vegetables
b. make or create

wound:
a. injury
b. wrapped or tied

wind:
a. wrap or tie
b. movement of air

bass:
a. deep or low sound
b. type of fish

NAME ______________________

Review Homophones and Multiple-Meaning Words

Complete each sentence with a homophone of the word in bold.

People have always **bin** ________________ interested in what the future **mite** ________________ hold. Books and movies that show what **hour** ________________ future lives will **bee** ________________ like are always popular. During the early 1980s, three houses of the future were built. These "Xanadu houses," were built in Florida, Wisconsin, and Tennessee. They were meant **two** ________________ showcase the latest technology and show people what their homes could look like one day.

Xanadu houses were **maid** ________________ of foam instead of concrete and **steal** ________________. **Dew** ________________ you **no** ________________ how to make a piñata? You cover a balloon with papier-mâché. When it dries, you pop the balloon, and the papier-mâché holds **it's** ________________ shape. This is the idea behind the construction of the Xanadu houses which looked like giant bubbles.

Inside, everything was run **buy** ________________ computers. You could set the bathtub to fill with water at a certain time of the day. Meals could be cooked automatically. The owners of a Xanadu house would even have a computerized chef to help them **chews** ________________ and prepare healthful meals. During the day, the beds vanished into the walls so there **wood** ________________ be more space.

At **there** ________________ **peek** ________________ of popularity, thousands of tourists visited the Xanadu houses. After a while, technology advanced, and the houses didn't. Even if you never had the **chants** ________________ to **sea** ________________ a Xanadu house in person, plenty of photos and information are available online.

NAME ______________________________

Review Homophones and Multiple-Meaning Words

Read the definitions and the sentences below. Make a check mark beside the sentence in which the bold word matches the definition.

1. **clip** *verb* to fasten

   _____ Did you **clip** the leash to the collar? _____ **Clip** the bottom off the bag.

2. **fair** *adj.* beautiful; pretty

   _____ Bessy won first prize at the state **fair**! _____ The **fair** maiden kissed the prince.

3. **league** *noun* a group of people

   _____ Have you ever read *20,000* ***Leagues*** *Under the Sea* by Jules Verne? _____ Carlos is in a soccer **league**.

4. **grave** *adj.* important; serious

   _____ The detective is in **grave** danger. _____ We visited the **grave**.

5. **rash** *noun* a skin irritation

   _____ The **rash** is from poison ivy. _____ Paul made a **rash** decision.

6. **tart** *adj.* sour

   _____ The lemonade is too **tart**. _____ I bought six berry **tarts**.

7. **racket** *noun* a paddle used in sports

   _____ Where is Libby's tennis **racket**? _____ Who is making that **racket**?

8. **bay** *noun* part of the sea

   _____ A **bay** leaf will flavor the soup. _____ The boat is in the **bay**.

9. **yard** *noun* 36 inches

   _____ Cara bought three **yards** of fabric. _____ The party will be held in Mr. Hammond's front **yard**.

NAME ____________________

Lesson 3.6 Acronyms and Initializations

Clipped words are often used in their shortened forms for convenience.

mathematics = math   referee = ref   gasoline = gas   teenager = teen

Write the word from the box that matches the bold clipped word beside it.

airplane	hamburgers	advertisement	bicycle	graduate
taxicab	dormitory	veterinarian	laboratories	statistics

From: adamson16@wiredlife.com
Date: July 17, 2007
To: pjsnyder@smallworld.com
Subject: How's life in Oregon?

Dear P.J.,

Last week, my family flew to Colorado to visit some schools Missy applied to. It's strange to think that next year my sister will be a high-school **grad** ________________. We took a **taxi** ________________ to the airport since our **plane** ________________ left so early in the morning. The **dorm** ________________ rooms were awfully small, but Missy was really impressed with the science **labs** ________________. Later on, we ate some **burgers** ________________ at the student union and talked to a few students.

My parents have finally decided that I'm old enough to ride my **bike** ________________ to Dr. Vega's office. He posted an **ad** ________________ asking for help a couple of days a week. He thinks it's great that I plan on being a **vet** ________________ one day and takes all my questions seriously.

Have you been to any ballgames? Are you keeping **stats** ________________ for your favorite players? I hope you're having a great summer.

Your friend,

Jared

NAME ______________________

Lesson 3.6 Acronyms and Initializations

Acronyms and **initializations** are abbreviations using the first letter of each word in a name or title. In an acronym, the letters are pronounced as a word (SCUBA). In an initialization, the individual letters are pronounced (SUV).

SCUBA = **s**elf-**c**ontained **u**nderwater **b**reathing **a**pparatus

SUV = **s**ports **u**tility **v**ehicle

In some acronyms or initializations, small words, like articles or prepositions, are left out. FBI = **F**ederal **B**ureau *of* **I**nvestigation

Read the sentences below. Replace each set of bold words with an acronym or initialization from the box.

UFO	MIA	NASA	CIA

1. The **Central Intelligence Agency** ________________ collects information about foreign governments and people and reports it to the U.S. government.
2. If you'd like to become an astronaut, look for some tips on the **National Aeronautics and Space Administration** ________________ Web site.
3. Marcus saw an **unidentified flying object** ________________ in his yard.
4. The purpose of the downtown memorial is to honor the soldiers who are **missing in action** ________________.

The initializations below are often used in casual e-mails to friends. Draw a line between each initialization and the words it represents.

1. FYI	by the way
2. LOL	in my opinion
3. TIA	as soon as possible
4. BTW	thanks in advance
5. ASAP	for your information
6. IMO	laughing out loud

NAME ______________________

Lesson 3.7 Word Play

A **palindrome** is a word or sentence that reads the same forward and backward.

refer	eve	solos
We sew.	Nurses run.	Did Hannah say as Hannah did?

Read the sentences and phrases below. On the line, write the word from the box that correctly completes each palindrome. You may want to use a piece of scrap paper to help you figure out which word is missing.

hid	like	odd	Adam	won	memos	Don't	frost
dine	am	war	Dr.	not	mayor	Anne	stinky

1. Now, sir, a ________________ is won.
2. ________________, I vote more cars race Rome to Vienna.
3. Derek, I ________________ red!
4. Are we ________________ drawn onward to new era?
5. Some men interpret nine ________________.
6. Stella ________________ no wallets.
7. Too bad, I ________________ a boot.
8. Gary knits a ________________ rag.
9. ________________ nod.
10. No mists or ________________, Simon.
11. Madam, I'm ________________.
12. Did I ________________, Enid? I did!
13. Roy, am I ________________?
14. ________________ Awkward
15. Ned, I ________________ a maiden.
16. Never ________________ or even.

NAME ______________________

Lesson 3.7 Word Play

A **portmanteau** (pôrt′ man tō′) word contains parts of two other words. Unlike a compound word, it contains only parts of the words, not the entire words.

gleam + shimmer = glimmer   motor + hotel = motel

Replace each set of bold words below with a portmanteau word from the box.

Internet	slathered	smog	glimmer	mopeds	brash
travelogue	flurry	brunch	splurge	humongous	

Any Thai **travel + monologue** ________________ is sure to mention the Chatuchak Market in Bangkok, Thailand. This **huge + monstrous** ________________ 35-acre market has about 9,000 booths. It is one of the biggest marketplaces in the world. On a typical weekend day, it has between 200,000 and 300,000 visitors.

Bargains are easy to find. Even though you may not be used to being **bold + rash** ________________, customers are expected to haggle for goods. Some people **splash + surge** ________________ on carved statues or valuable antiques. Others are happy to buy smaller trinkets, like masks, teacups, dolls, or brightly-colored fish.

Make sure that you take the time to soak in the fast-paced atmosphere. **Motor + pedals** ________________ weave in and out of the crowds. Displays of beautiful jewelry **glitter + shimmer** ________________ in the sun. Try stopping for **breakfast + lunch** ________________ at one of the corner stands. Have some noodles **slapped + lathered** ________________ with a traditional Thai sauce. On a cloudy day, there may be some morning **smoke + fog** ________________, but the sun is sure to quickly burn it off.

There are many pictures of Chatuchak Market available on the **international + network** ________________, but none of them can truly capture the **flutter + hurry** ________________ of activity or the sights and sounds of the real thing.

NAME ___________________________

Review Clipped Words, Acronyms, and Word Play

On the line, write a clipped word for each word or set of words in bold.

1. Roma and Brady placed an **advertisement** ____________ in the paper for the yard sale they planned to have on Saturday.
2. When Roma was cleaning the basement, she found her old toy **refrigerator** ____________, complete with milk bottles, fruit, and plastic **hamburgers** ____________.
3. Brady was going to sell some stuffed animals he had bought on a long-ago field trip to the **zoological garden** ____________.
4. Roma thought about selling her **miniature** ____________ chemistry **laboratory** ____________, but decided she might use it again someday.
5. Brady's brother wanted to sell his old **bicycle** ____________.
6. The first customers on the day of the sale were a group of **teenagers** ____________ who were friends with Brady's brother.
7. At the end of the day, Mrs. Dimitru took a **photograph** ____________ of Roma and Brady grinning at the camera and holding a very full cash box.

On the line, write an acronym or initialization for each set of words.

1. grade point average ____________
2. very important person ____________
3. Internal Revenue Service ____________
4. also known as ____________
5. automated teller machine ____________
6. self-contained underwater breathing apparatus ____________

NAME ______________________________

Review Clipped Words, Acronyms, and Word Play

Make a check mark beside the palindrome in each pair below.

1. ______ A man, a plan, a canal, Panama! ______ Red roots are put up to order.
2. ______ Sages can use gas. ______ We'll let Dad tell Lew.
3. ______ No lemon, and no melon. ______ Wontons? Not now.
4. ______ Delia sailed, Eva waved, Elias ailed. ______ Pals can slap.
5. ______ Was it Elliot's toilets I saw? ______ Race fast, safe car.

Use the words in the box to solve the problems below.

Muppet	sting	camera	poodle	infomercial	sportscast	boom	crunch

1. pain + ____________________ = pang
2. information + commercial = ____________________
3. ____________________ + recorder = camcorder
4. Labrador + ____________________ = labradoodle
5. ____________________ + hoist = boost
6. squeeze + ____________________ = scrunch
7. sports + broadcast = ____________________
8. marionette + puppet = ____________________

On the lines below, create three portmanteau words of your own.

____________________ ____________________ ____________________

Phonics Connection

1. Which word in the first exercise has the soft **g** sound? ____________________
2. Which word in the first exercise has the soft **c** sound? ____________________

REVIEW: CHAPTER 3 LESSONS 6–7

NAME ______________________

Lesson 3.8 Figures of Speech

A **simile** is a comparison of two unlike things using the words *like* or *as.*

The newborn puppy's *ears were as soft as velvet.*

The *music was like a hammer* thumping at Carla's door.

Read the sentences below. Underline each simile you find, and circle the word or words that indicate it is a simile.

1. Once the storm had passed, the sea was as smooth as glass.
2. In the sun, Maureen's hair was as bright and shiny as a new copper penny.
3. After staying up so late the night before, Bailey moved as slowly as a snail on Saturday morning.
4. The secret was like a heavy weight that Damian carried on his shoulders.
5. When the water had boiled, the teakettle whistled like a cheerful bird on a spring morning.
6. Lola's heart dropped like a stone as she watched her father read her report card.

Circle the two things being compared in each simile below.

1. The tiny bits of confetti drifted to the floor like multicolored snowflakes.
2. After returning from the stylist, Amanda's hair was as curly as a poodle's.
3. Wearing all of his hockey gear, Julio looked like a turtle gliding on ice.
4. The desert cacti looked like soldiers saluting us as we drove past them.
5. After hiking all day yesterday, my legs feel as stiff as tree trunks today.
6. The hawk hovered in one place, riding the wind like a kite held tight by string.
7. My grandmother told me that whenever I visit, she feels as young and energetic as a kitten.

NAME ______________________

Lesson 3.8 Figures of Speech

A **metaphor** is a comparison of two unlike things without using *like* or *as.*

The *murmuring of his parents in the next room was a lullaby* that quickly put Ari to sleep.

Read the paragraphs below. Find and underline the seven metaphors.

On the morning of the play, the smell of freshly baked muffins danced through Meena's bedroom. As she awoke, she could still see the moon through the curtains, a thin silvery smile in the aqua sky. Meena stretched and lazily reached for her glasses. Suddenly, she sat straight up in bed. She remembered with a shock that today was the day of the play. She lay back down and buried her face in her pillow.

Meena must have drifted back to sleep, because some time later, she awoke again. A soothing hand on her forehead was a cool towel wiping away her worries. Meena's mom sat on the edge of the bed. She held a muffin and a mug of warm tea. The sari she wore was a puddle of brilliant blue on the bed.

"Today's the big day," said Mrs. Singh. "How do you feel?"

Meena sighed. "Terrible. When I woke up earlier, I couldn't remember a single one of my lines." Mrs. Singh looked at her daughter for a moment and then grabbed the dog-eared script from Meena's desk. She read one of Meena's cues, and without thinking, Meena recited her first speech perfectly. The sun was a spotlight, shining through the window and illuminating Meena and her smile of relief.

Mrs. Singh patted her daughter's hand and stood up. "Listening to you recite Shakespeare is music to my ears," she said. "You're going to be a hit."

NAME ______________________

Lesson 3.8 Figures of Speech

Read each sentence below. The word in parentheses will tell you whether you should complete the sentence with a simile or a metaphor.

1. The rolling green hills stretched out across the landscape like

   ______________________ . (simile)

2. The waves were ______________________ that beckoned Chloe to come and play. (metaphor)

3. The dog's shrill barks were ______________________ to Mrs. Blum as she tossed and turned in bed. (metaphor)

4. "This headache feels like ______________________ !" exclaimed Alyssa, cradling her head in her hands. (simile)

5. In the summertime, freckles seem to cover Maggie's face like

   ______________________ . (simile)

The similes below are mixed up. Replace each bold word with a word or phrase from the box that makes sense in the comparison.

mule	bee	wink	bird	board	bone	feather	glove

1. dry as a **pool** ______________
2. fits like a **jacket** ______________
3. quick as a **wave** ______________
4. eats like a **spoon** ______________
5. light as a **brick** ______________
6. stubborn as a **car** ______________
7. busy as a **koala bear** ______________
8. stiff as a **cushion** ______________

NAME ______________________________

Lesson 3.8 Figures of Speech

Read each sentence below. If it contains a metaphor, circle **M**. If it contains a simile, circle **S**.

1. **M S** The sad news was a cloud that hung over our house all week long.
2. **M S** The basement was a time capsule, full of family souvenirs.
3. **M S** The fire roared like a wild beast as the firefighters attacked it.
4. **M S** His grandpa's praise was a treasure that Marquis carefully guarded.
5. **M S** The hound's howls were like a siren alerting his family to danger.

Read the paragraphs below. Underline the four similes and circle the five metaphors.

Tick-tock, tick-tock. Hannah bounced back and forth from one foot to the other, a clock counting down the seconds. She raised her racket and smacked the ball, sending it across the net like a rocket blasting through space.

Quickly, Hannah dashed to center court and waited, knees slightly bent. She was a lioness waiting patiently in the tall grass for her prey to come bounding back over the net. Hannah's opponent swung at the flying ball. His racket made a perfect arc around his body like a tetherball tied to a pole. He connected with the ball and turned it into yellow lightning that streaked back in the other direction.

In a flash, Hannah leaped to her left as suddenly as if some giant hand had yanked her sideways. She cranked her arm backward, setting the spring on a powerful catapult that sent the ball flying away from her.

The ball ricocheted between the two opponents for the next few minutes. The court echoed with a sound like popcorn popping in slow motion. Finally, Hannah directed the tennis ball to the far-left corner. Her opponent ran but arrived just in time to see it bounce away, a bus pulling from the curb with its doors closed.

"Good game, Dad!" Hannah yelled across the net.

NAME ______________________________

Lesson 3.9 Idioms

A group of words that mean something other than what they appear to mean is called an **idiom**. In the sentence that follows, Sarah and her mom are able to make a compromise.

> Sarah and her mom were able to *meet halfway* and work out an agreement.

Draw a line to match each idiom in column 1 to its definition in column 2.

1. got the ball rolling	received all the attention
2. cutting corners	to act slowly or reluctantly
3. hit the hay	took a risk
4. spill the beans	taking shortcuts
5. drag one's heels	tell a secret
6. to cave in	to give up
7. stuck her neck out	go to bed
8. pull your own weight	got things started
9. stole the spotlight	to do your share

Underline the idiom in each sentence below.

1. Krista has a green thumb, so her garden was a great success this summer.
2. Once you know the ropes, you'll have no trouble finding your way around.
3. Mr. Wasserman's new car was a lemon, so he was lucky to have a warranty.
4. "You're skating on thin ice," Tara told her daughter.
5. Caleb and David were horsing around in the kitchen when the lamp broke.
6. Dad is usually all thumbs, but he did put the vacuum back together again.
7. The surprise party is on Saturday, so don't let the cat out of the bag.

NAME ______________________

Lesson 3.9 Idioms

Read each idiom and definition below. On the line that follows, write a sentence using the idiom.

1. read between the lines = understand something even if it's not obvious

 ____

2. stand one's ground = defend one's position

 ____

3. go back to square one = start from the beginning

 ____

4. a piece of cake = something that's very easy

 ____

5. cost an arm and a leg = very expensive

 ____

6. get on one's nerves = irritate or annoy someone

 ____

7. know something backward and forward = know something very well

 ____

Phonics Connection

Use the idioms in the exercise above to complete the items below.

1. On the lines, write two words in which the long **e** sound is spelled differently.

 ____________ ____________

2. On the lines, write two words in which **s** makes the /z/ sound.

 ____________ ____________

NAME ______________________________

Lesson 3.10 Analogies

An **analogy** shows a relationship between two pairs of words. To understand an analogy, it is important to figure out how the words relate to one another.

- *Finger* is to *hand* as *page* is to *book*.
  A finger is part of a hand, the way a page is part of a book.
- *Paintbrush* is to *artist* as *microscope* is to *scientist*.
  A paintbrush is an artist's tool as a microscope is a scientist's tool.
- *Grass* is to *grasses* as *mouse* is to *mice*.
  Grasses is the plural form of *grass*, as *mice* is the plural form of *mouse*.

Sometimes, analogies are written in the following way—eat : ate :: run : ran.
To read this analogy, you would say, "*Eat* is to *ate* as *run* is to *ran*."

Complete each analogy below with a word from the box. Remember to figure out how the words are related before you look for the missing word.

state	dog	roar	apple	hospital	ugly	evening	seven	children

1. *Beautiful* is to ____________________ as *wide* is to *narrow*.
2. *Lunch* is to *afternoon* as *dinner* is to ____________________ .
3. *Tomato* is to *tomatoes* as *child* is to ____________________ .
4. *Soldier* is to *army* as ____________________ is to *country*.
5. ____________________ is to *fruit* as *spinach* is to *vegetable*.
6. *Two* is to *four* as ____________________ is to *fourteen*.
7. *Snake* is to *hiss* as *lion* is to ____________________ .
8. *Poodle* is to ____________________ as *Siamese* is to *cat*.

On the lines below, write two analogies of your own.

1. ____________________ is to ____________________ as ____________________ is to ____________________ .

2. ____________________ is to ____________________ as ____________________ is to ____________________ .

NAME ______________________________

Lesson 3.10 Analogies

Read each analogy below. Unscramble the bold word, and write it on the line to complete the analogy.

1. *Blender* is to *mix* as *oven* is to **bkea** ____________________ .
2. *Legal* is to *illegal* as **mssye** ____________________ is to *neat.*
3. **ngik** ____________________ is to *queen* as *prince* is to *princess.*
4. *Nickel* is to **llador** ____________________ as *inch* is to *foot.*
5. *Flour* is to **erfwlo** ____________________ as *mussels* is to *muscles.*
6. *Clock* is to **eitm** ____________________ as *thermometer* is *temperature.*
7. *Slap* is to *slapping* as *kiss* is to **ssinkig** ____________________ .
8. **zzaj** ____________________ is to *music* as *waltz* is to *dance.*

Replace each picture below with a word that correctly completes the analogy.

1. ____________________ : south :: answer : question
2. ____________________ : swimmer :: track : runner
3. knife : cut :: 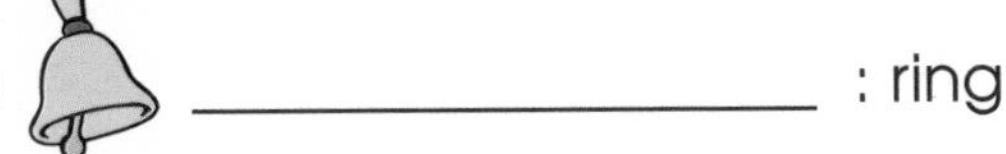 ____________________ : ring
4. ____________________ : cure :: teacher : teach
5. bud : bloom :: caterpillar :  ____________________
6. tongue : taste :: 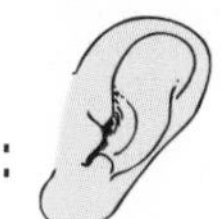 ____________________ : hear

NAME ______________________

Lesson 3.10 Analogies

Read each analogy below. On the line, explain how the words are related.

Ex.: *Money* is to *billfold* as *milk* is to *refrigerator*.
Money is kept in a billfold as milk is kept in a refrigerator.

1. *Chef* is to *cook* as *author* is to *write*.

   ____

2. *Neigh* is to *horse* as *meow* is to *cat*.

   ____

3. *Yolk* is to *egg* as *core* is to *apple*.

   ____

4. *Boring* is to *exciting* as *cheap* is to *expensive*.

   ____

5. *Pair* is to *pear* as *serial* is to *cereal*.

   ____

6. *Second* is to *minute* as *ounce* is to *pound*.

   ____

The analogies below are incomplete. Chose the word from the pair in parentheses that best completes each analogy, and underline it.

1. *Loose* is to (tight, loosen) as *shout* is to *whisper*.
2. *Katie* is to (name, Katherine) as *Jim* is to *James*.
3. (Cold, Preheat) is to *heat* as *misjudge* is to *judge*.
4. *Bird* is to *nest* as *bee* is to (hive, honey).
5. *Fifty-two* is to *twenty-five* as (one hundred, eighteen) is to *eighty-one*.
6. *Raise* is to (increase, decrease) as *mistake* is to *error*.
7. (Trumpet, Key) is to *piano* as *steering wheel* is to *car*.
8. *Herd* is to *buffalo* as (goose, flock) is to *geese*.

NAME ________________________

Lesson 3.10 Analogies

The following analogies are out of order. Use the hints in line 2 of each analogy to help you place the words in the correct order.

1. *Weight* is to *temperature* as *scale* is to *thermometer.*

   Temperature is to ________________ as *weight* is to ________________ .

2. *Golfer* is to *bat* as *baseball player* is to *golf club.*

   ________________ is to *baseball player* as *golf club* is to ________________ .

3. *Keyboard* is to *eraser* as *delete* is to *pencil.*

   Eraser is to ________________ as ________________ is to *keyboard.*

4. *September* is to *Tuesday* as *Monday* is to *August.*

   ________________ is to *Tuesday* as *August* is to ________________ .

5. *Smile* is to *sad* as *happy* is to *frown.*

   ________________ is to *happy* as ________________ is to *sad.*

6. *Nail* is to *thread* as *needle* is to *hammer.*

   ________________ is to *nail* as ________________ is to *thread.*

7. *Hot* is to *boiling* as *freezing* is to *cold.*

   Cold is to ________________ as ________________ is to *boiling.*

8. *School* is to *government* as *politician* is to *student.*

   Politician is to ________________ as *student* is to ________________ .

9. *Coach* is to *orchestra* as *conductor* is to *basketball team.*

   ________________ is to *orchestra* as *coach* is to ________________ .

10. *Bank* is to *university* as *money* is to *knowledge.*

    ________________ is to *bank* as ________________ is to *university.*

NAME ____________________

Review Figures of Speech, Idioms, and Analogies

Read the sentences below. Find the figure of speech in each sentence and underline it. On the first line, write **S** if the comparison is a simile and **M** if it is a metaphor. On the the second line, tell which two things are being compared.

1. Homesickness washed over Maddy like a wave as her parents drove away.

_____ ______________________________

2. Carter was a monkey as he quickly and nimbly climbed the tree.

_____ ______________________________

3. During his dentist appointment, the novocaine made Dakota's tongue feel like a big wad of cotton in his mouth.

_____ ______________________________

4. When the air-conditioner gave out, the classroom became as hot as an oven.

_____ ______________________________

5. Even viewed through the powerful telescope, Mars looked like a tiny red marble fixed in the night sky.

_____ ______________________________

6. *Life is a journey* is Mr. Applebaum's favorite saying.

_____ ______________________________

7. After the blizzard, the backyard was transformed into a magical wonderland.

_____ ______________________________

On the lines below, write two similes and two metaphors of your own.

1. ______________________________

2. ______________________________

3. ______________________________

4. ______________________________

REVIEW: CHAPTER 3 LESSONS 8–10

NAME ______________________

Review Figures of Speech, Idioms, and Analogies

Read each idiom in column 1. On the line, write the letter of the matching definition from column 2.

1. _____ to twist someone's arm
2. _____ a pain in the neck
3. _____ lend someone a hand
4. _____ keep one's chin up
5. _____ to have one's hands full
6. _____ grab a bite
7. _____ by the skin of one's teeth
8. _____ all ears
9. _____ keep your eye on the ball

a. to be very busy
b. ready to listen
c. something that is annoying
d. eat something
e. pay close attention
f. just barely
g. help out
h. to try to convince someone
i. keep a positive attitude

Complete each analogy below with a word from the box.

help	star	tame	racket	grasshopper	summer	woman	fantastic

1. women : _______________ :: planes : plane
2. musician : band :: _______________ : constellation
3. _______________ : wild :: under : over
4. _______________ : tennis :: stick : hockey
5. pretty : gorgeous :: good : _______________
6. banana : fruit :: _______________ : insect
7. _______________ : helpful :: joy : joyful
8. June: _______________ :: December : winter

REVIEW: CHAPTER 3 LESSONS 8–10

NAME ___________________________

Lesson 4.1 Guide Words

Guide words, found at the top of a dictionary page, tell you the first and last word on that page. If the word you are searching for comes between the guide words in alphabetical order, it will be on that page of the dictionary.

For example, *pincushion* would be on the page that has the guide words *pillar* and *piranha* because it comes between them in alphabetical order.

Read each pair of guide words and the set of words listed below them. Underline each word in the set that could be found on the same dictionary page as the pair of guide words.

sage • sandpaper	legislation • library
satisfaction	lemon
saleswoman	licorice
sacred	legendary
saliva	lesson
sandal	leotard
sardine	lengthwise

Look up each of the following words in a dictionary. On the lines, write the guide words from the page on which you found the word.

1. bridegroom ____________ ____________
2. grouchy ____________ ____________
3. mathematics ____________ ____________
4. hasty ____________ ____________
5. pigtail ____________ ____________
6. serene ____________ ____________
7. publish ____________ ____________

NAME ___________________________

Lesson 4.1 Guide Words

Read the following sentences. Circle the letter beside the pair of guide words that would be found on the same dictionary page as the bold word.

1. The WNBA, or Women's National Basketball **Association**, was formed in 1996.

   a. asleep • assume b. assorted • astronomy

2. The regular season begins in the **summer** when the NBA season has ended.

   a. summon • superior b. suitcase • sunglasses

3. Many people are surprised to learn that it was not the first women's **professional** basketball league in the country.

   a. print • product b. producer • project

4. The WBL played **three** seasons, from 1978 through 1981.

   a. threat • thunder b. threw • thyme

5. Currently, the WNBA's 14 teams are divided into two **conferences**.

   a. confetti • connect b. conditioner • confuse

6. Penny Toler was the first woman to **score** a point in the WNBA.

   a. scorpion • scribble b. scheme • scowl

7. Sheryl Swoopes is one of the most respected female **basketball** players.

   a. bark • bassoon b. bargain • basis

8. She has more than 2,000 **career** points and has a shoe named after her.

   a. cardinal • cartoon b. cargo • cashier

9. Swoopes was a member of the U. S. women's basketball team when it won an **Olympic** gold medal in 1996.

   a. omelet • opinion b. offend • onion

10. Lisa Leslie, who is 6 feet 5 **inches** tall, was the first WNBA player to dunk.

    a. inaccurate • income b. impress • incense

11. Leslie played for the Los Angeles Sparks **during** the WNBA's first season.

    a. drummer • dune b. dungeon • dynamic

NAME ______________________

Lesson 4.2 Entry Words

When you look for a word in a dictionary, you are looking for an **entry word**. Entry words, usually printed in bold, are often base words. For example, you'd look for *safe*, not *safely*, *explain*, not *explaining*, and *cherry*, not *cherries*.

entry word | pronunciation & syllables | part of speech | meaning

nuisance (nū′ səns) *noun* something that is annoying

Circle the word in each set below that is most likely to be an entry word.

1. driest	mayonnaise	intersections
2. nutshells	locomotive	mysteries
3. husky	located	peacefully
4. windier	misleading	beaver

Use the dictionary entries below to answer the questions that follow.

flounder (floun′ dər) 1. *verb* to struggle or move clumsily
2. *noun* a type of fish

mystery (mis′ tə rē) *noun, plural* ***mysteries*** something strange or unexplained

respectful (ri spekt′ fəl) *adj.* showing respect, *adv.* respectfully

1. How many syllables are there in *respectful*? ______________
2. What is the plural form of *mystery*? ______________
3. Write two sentences using the different meanings for the word *flounder*.

____

____

4. Which syllable is stressed in *mystery*? ______________
5. Is *respectfully* an entry word? ______________

NAME ______________________________

Lesson 4.2 Entry Words

Read the paragraphs below. On the line beside each bold word, write the entry word you would look for in a dictionary.

Only five miles long by eight miles wide, Gee's Bend lies at a curve in the Alabama River. Because it is so **isolated** ________________, this small town is unique. For many years, there was no ferry service to take the **residents** ________________ of Gee's Bend across the river. Most of the 750 or so people who live in Gee's Bend are African American. Many are **descendants** ________________ of the slaves who originally **worked** ________________ on the plantation there. The town is rich in the history and culture of the **families** ________________ that have **lived** ________________ there since before the Civil War.

Gee's Bend has become more **widely** ________________ known during the last few years because of some very interesting quilts. **Quilting** ________________ has been **recognized** ________________ as a type of folk art that is both useful and beautiful. But the quilts of Gee's Bend have **attracted** ________________ attention for some other reasons too. Experts have been very **impressed** ________________ by the creativity and **inventiveness** ________________ of the patterns. As a result, the quilts have been **creating** ________________ a bit of a stir in the art world.

An exhibit of 60 quilts was **displayed** ________________ at the Museum of Fine Arts in Houston and the Whitney Museum of American Art in New York. The quilts were **stitched** ________________ by 42 **women** ________________ from 4 different **generations** ________________. Whether the quilts are viewed as works of art or just beautiful blankets, they are an important part of the history of Gee's Bend.

NAME ______________________

Review Guide Words and Entry Words

Read each pair of guide words below. On the line, write the letter of the word you would find on a dictionary page with those guide words.

	Guide words	a.	b.	c.
1. _____	oil * onshore	a. ogre	b. olive	c. offer
2. _____	sheath * shipment	a. shepherd	b. shock	c. shiver
3. _____	grapefruit * greasy	a. grateful	b. granola	c. greenhouse
4. _____	lettuce * lifelike	a. lightning	b. lentil	c. lifeguard
5. _____	disability * discard	a. disgust	b. disaster	c. director
6. _____	portico * postal	a. possess	b. postman	c. potluck
7. _____	treaty * trillion	a. treatment	b. treasure	c. triangle
8. _____	milestone * mimic	a. mildew	b. mill	c. might
9. _____	reporter * research	a. require	b. repeat	c. resource
10. _____	glaze * gnarled	a. gobble	b. global	c. godparent
11. _____	essay * etiquette	a. eucalyptus	b. ethnic	c. erupt
12. _____	yesterday * your	a. yolk	b. yourself	c. yes
13. _____	flicker * flour	a. flow	b. fluffy	c. flinch
14. _____	apricot * archery	a. approve	b. arbor	c. archway
15. _____	rodent * romance	a. rolling pin	b. rooster	c. romp

Each heading below is a set of guidewords from a dictionary page. Write the words from the box under the correct headings.

nomination nightingale nosebleed nickel noise nosy north newsstand noodle

newscast * nimble	ninety * nook	noon * notation
__________	__________	__________
__________	__________	__________
__________	__________	__________

NAME ______________________________

Review Guide Words and Entry Words

Write the entry words for the words listed below in the numbered spaces in the crossword puzzle.

Across

4. waltzes
5. geese
7. friendliest
10. cloudier
11. kilometers

Down

1. plugging
2. nuttiest
3. happiness
6. straighten
8. adored
9. echoes

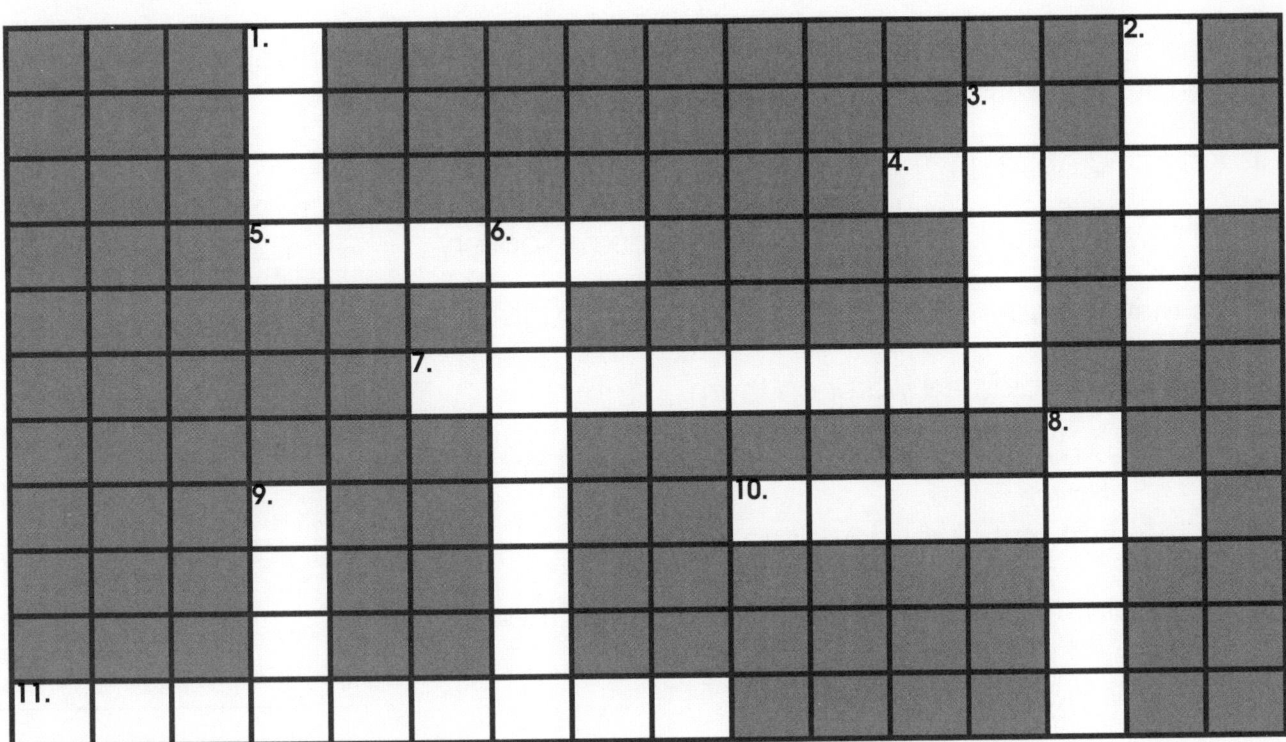

REVIEW: CHAPTER 4 LESSONS 1–2

Use the dictionary entries below to answer the questions that follow.

diamond (dī′ mənd) 1. *noun* a baseball infield
2. *noun* a valuable mineral used in making jewelry

digest (dī jest′) *verb* to break down food so that it can be used by the body

1. Which definition of *diamond* is used in this sentence?
The antique ring had three tiny diamonds and a small ruby. ______________

2. Which syllable is stressed in *digest*? ______________

3. What part of speech is *diamond* when it means *a baseball infield*? ______________

4. What would the entry word be for *digested*? ______________

NAME ______________________

Lesson 4.3 Word Families

A **word family** is a group of words that have the same base word. Prefixes, suffixes, and endings can be added to a base word to create word families.

base word: **agree** dis**agree**, **agree**able, **agree**ing, dis**agree**ment
base word: **judge** **judg**ing, **judge**ment, **judge**s, mis**judge**, **judge**d
base word: **straight** **straight**en, **straight**er, **straight**est

Read the sentences below. For each bold word, think of two other words in the same word family and write them on the lines.

1. Kelly and Abby gave a **friendly** wave to Mrs. Milivich, who was sweeping the front walk outside her bakery. ______________ ______________
2. As they turned the corner, a truck drove through a puddle and **rudely** splashed water on them. ______________ ______________
3. The girls glanced at each other and **erupted** into giggles at the sight of their muddy, dripping clothes. ______________ ______________
4. Seconds later, Mrs. Milivich **appeared** beside them, clucking and fussing like a mother hen. ______________ ______________
5. "Why don't you girls come inside and we'll get you **cleaned** up?" she suggested. ______________ ______________
6. Kelly and Abby followed Mrs. Milivich inside the sweet-smelling, **spotless** store. ______________ ______________
7. Kelly inhaled **deeply** and grinned as she accepted the towel that Mrs. Milivich offered her. ______________ ______________
8. When the girls left the bakery, they each carried a loaf of bread and a cookie studded with **semisweet** chocolate chips. ______________ ______________

NAME ______________________________

Lesson 4.3 Word Families

Read the clues below. Each clue is followed by three words from the same word family. Circle the letter of the word that matches the clue.

1. without clouds
   - **a.** cloudless **b.** cloudy **c.** cloudiest
2. able to be broken
   - **a.** breakdown **b.** breaks **c.** breakable
3. below consciousness
   - **a.** consciously **b.** subconscious **c.** consciousness
4. full of play
   - **a.** playful **b.** playing **c.** playground
5. not natural
   - **a.** unnatural **b.** supernatural **c.** naturally
6. dividing in two
   - **a.** splits **b.** split **c.** splitting
7. not responsive
   - **a.** nonresponsive **b.** responding **c.** responds
8. between nations
   - **a.** nationally **b.** nations **c.** international
9. a ceremony for people who have completed a level of schooling
   - **a.** postgraduate **b.** graduation **c.** graduates

Phonics Connection

1. On the lines, write one word from the exercise above in which **ci** makes the /sh/ sound and one word in which **ti** makes the /sh/ sound.

   ____________________ ____________________

2. Circle all the words in the exercise above that contain the hard **g** sound.

NAME ______________________________

Lesson 4.3 Word Families

Read the following paragraphs. Circle the words that belong to the word families *ski*, *snow*, and *move*. Then, write each word in the correct column following the selection. You do not need to circle the same word twice.

I stood at the top of Mount Houston, unmoving as I watched snowflakes drift quietly to the ground. Bundled up in my skiwear, I was plenty warm and in no hurry. I knew that my skis would carry me quickly down the snowy mountainside. I removed my goggles for a moment so I could get a better look at the snowcapped mountains surrounding me. Even though I had skied many times before, the beauty of the mountains still moved me.

Yesterday, a snowstorm blew in and covered everything with a fresh layer of white. Heavy, powdery snowfall like that provides the best skiing conditions. It makes moving down the slopes a breeze. Luckily, though, if I do fall, my skis are easily removable.

Last month, I met a woman who lives here all year, but she isn't a skier. She prefers walking through the forests wearing snowshoes. A few days ago, I joined her on a hike. It was snowing that day, and bundled in my snowsuit, normal movement was difficult. Although my new friend moves easily while wearing those big, flat shoes, I had a hard time tromping across the snowdrifts. It was quite a workout!

move: ______________ ______________ ______________

______________ ______________ ______________

____

snow: ______________ ______________ ______________

______________ ______________ ______________

______________ ______________ ______________

ski: ______________ ______________ ______________

______________ ______________

NAME ______________________

Lesson 4.3 Word Families

How many word-family members can you create for each word listed below?

cover		joy		create	
______	______	______	______	______	______
______	______	______	______	______	______
______	______	______	______	______	______
______	______	______	______	______	______
______	______	______	______	______	______
______	______	______	______	______	______

One member of each word family listed below is a incorrect. Circle the word in each group that does not belong. Use a dictionary if you need help.

1.	unspeakable	speakability	speakers	misspeaking
2.	unwatched	watching	prewatched	watchfulness
3.	undervalued	valuable	invaluable	valuelessly
4.	readability	misread	unreading	reads
5.	unknowabled	acknowledge	unknowing	knowledgeable
6.	misinformation	informing	malinformed	informational
7.	flaming	inflammation	flammable	disinflamed
8.	managist	unmanageable	managerial	mismanaged
9.	enfold	foldness	unfolded	refolding
10.	needlessier	neediest	unneeded	needfulness
11.	behavior	unbehavely	behaving	misbehaved
12.	mishearing	hearingly	rehear	unheard
13.	stableness	destabilized	restabled	unstable
14.	specialty	specializes	specialist	speciallessly

NAME ______________________________

Lesson 4.4 Word Origins

Many words in the English language have Greek or Latin roots. Knowing what these roots mean can help you find the meanings of many unfamiliar words.

Latin		Greek	
aud = hear	(**aud**io)	**chron** = time	(**chron**icle)
vid, vis = see	(**vis**ion)	**bio** = life	(**bio**nic)
mar = sea	(**mar**ine)	**cycl** = circle, ring	(re**cycl**e)

Read each clue in column 1. On the line, write the letter of the word that matches the clue in column 2.

1. ______ an underwater ship	a. mariner
2. ______ the story of a person's life	b. audible
3. ______ a vehicle that has two circular wheels, a seat, and two pedals	c. biology
4. ______ able to be seen	d. chronological
5. ______ a sailor or person who navigates a ship	e. cyclone
6. ______ loud enough to be heard	f. evidence
7. ______ the study of living things	g. audience
8. ______ arranged in the order of time in which each thing happened	h. submarine
9. ______ a cassette that can be seen or viewed on a television screen	i. visible
10. ______ a storm, like a tornado, in which the wind blows in spirals or rings	j. bicycle
11. ______ a group of people gathered in one place to see or hear something	k. videocassette
12. ______ facts that help one see the answer or the truth	l. biography

NAME ____________________

Lesson 4.4 Word Origins

Latin		Greek	
ped = foot	(**ped**al)	**geo** = earth	(**geo**logy)
ann, enn = year	(**ann**ual)	**phon** = sound	(**phon**ograph)
liber = free	(**liber**ty)	**therm** = heat	(**therm**os)
aqua = water	(**aqua**tic)	**meter** = measure	(kilo**meter**)

Read the sentences below. Underline the Greek or Latin root from the pair in parentheses that will correctly complete the bold word.

1. Laura looked through her program as the **sym**__________________**y** warmed up in the orchestra pit. (meter, phon)
2. On Tuesday, my grandparents will be celebrating their 38th wedding __________________**iversary**. (ann, aqua)
3. When Kayla and I studied for our __________________**graphy** test, we memorized the capitals of all 50 states. (geo, therm)
4. A yellow, diamond-shaped sign tells drivers to slow down for a __________________**estrian** crossing. (liber, ped)
5. The car's **speedo**__________________ was not working, so Dad had no idea how fast he was going when the police officer stopped him. (phon, meter)
6. Joey packed his ski goggles, a down-filled jacket, sunscreen, and two pairs of __________________**al** underwear to keep him warm on the slopes. (therm, liber)
7. During the campaign, the students were allowed to watch a debate between the conservative and the __________________**al** candidates. (ped, liber)
8. Caring for a saltwater __________________**rium** can be a lot of work. (aqua, therm)
9. **Homo**__________________**es**, like *vane* and *vein*, are words that sound alike but are spelled differently. (ped, phon)
10. "Does a **centi**__________________**e** really have one hundred legs?" (meter, ped)

NAME ___________________________

Lesson 4.4 Word Origins

Latin		Greek	
port = carry	(trans**port**)	**graph** = write	(auto**graph**)
rupt = break	(e**rupt**)	**scope** = see	(micro**scope**)
scrib, **script** = write	(in**scrib**e)	**man** = hand	(**man**ual)
struct = build	(con**struct**)	**ast** = star	(**ast**eroid)

Choose the word from the box that matches each clue, and write it on the line. Circle the Greek or Latin root and find the word in the word search puzzle.

asterisk	interrupt	biography	astronomy	describe	export	manuscript	transport

1. to move something from one place to another ____________
2. a star-shaped symbol on a computer keyboard ____________
3. to tell about or give details about something ____________
4. to send to another country for trade ____________
5. a book written about a person's life ____________
6. to stop or break into something, like a conversation ____________
7. the study of stars ____________
8. something, such as a book, that is written ____________

i	k	v	h	w	e	b	i	o	g	r	a	p	h	y
n	r	h	n	s	p	p	r	e	m	m	s	t	q	a
t	q	m	a	n	u	s	c	r	i	p	t	p	k	s
e	p	e	h	n	f	f	u	r	e	q	r	h	r	t
r	t	g	t	u	i	m	e	a	x	g	o	v	d	e
r	i	d	e	u	p	l	r	t	p	b	n	f	a	r
u	t	w	r	b	d	y	w	e	o	r	o	h	d	i
p	t	t	r	a	n	s	p	o	r	t	m	l	o	s
t	d	e	s	c	r	i	b	e	t	e	y	b	b	k

NAME ____________________

Lesson 4.4 Word Origins

The Greek root **ology** means *the science of* or *the study of.*

zo**ology** = the study of animals   bi**ology** = the study of living things

Draw a line to match each word in column 1 with its meaning in column 2. Use the Greek and Latin roots you have already learned to help you determine the meanings of the words.

1. sociology	the study of crime
2. mythology	the study of radiation
3. musicology	the study of music
4. criminology	the study or science of bacteria
5. radiology	the study of cosmetics and beauty
6. cosmetology	the study of society
7. bacteriology	the study of myths

Complete each sentence below.

1. *Cardio* means *heart,* so *cardiology* is ____________________.

2. *Psych* means *mind,* so *psychology* is ____________________.

3. *Ornis* means *bird,* so *ornithology* is ____________________.

4. *Derma* means *skin,* so *dermatology* is ____________________.

5. *Cosm* means *universe,* so *cosmology* is ____________________.

6. *Herpeton* means *reptile,* so *herpetology* is ____________________.

Phonics Connection

Use the words in the first exercise to answer the questions below.

1. Which two words contain the short **i** sound spelled **y**?

____________________   ____________________

2. Circle the words that contain the hard **c** sound.

NAME ______________________

Review Word Families and Word Origins

The diary entries below contain seven pairs of words from different word families in bold. Group all seven pairs together and write them on the lines that follow.

May 8: I volunteered at the animal shelter today. I hate it when people are **irresponsible** and don't take good **care** of their animals. The animals are so **helpless**, and I want to do everything I can to make their lives better.

May 9: Brody's surprise party is on Saturday. I have to be **careful** I don't let the secret slip before then!

May 11: My mint-chip brownies were a great **success** at the bake sale. All three dozen sold during the first half-hour of the sale!

May 12: My little sister loves **performing** in front of people. At Aunt Helen's wedding, she sang two songs in front of nearly one hundred people!

May 14: Ms. Kovitch said that it would be **helpful** to study for the **history** test with a partner, so Crystal and I are going to quiz each other tonight.

May 15: The talent show is next week. Julia and I are **responsible** for planning the **refreshments** that will be served after the **performance**.

May 16: We made smoothies with **fresh** berries, bananas, and yogurt. Yum!

May 19: Terence and I tried the first of our science experiments today. It was **unsuccessful**, but we know what to do differently next time.

May 20: I visited Marissa's house today. It is on our town's register of **historic** places. The house has been in Marissa's family for 130 years!

1. ______________________ ______________________
2. ______________________ ______________________
3. ______________________ ______________________
4. ______________________ ______________________
5. ______________________ ______________________
6. ______________________ ______________________
7. ______________________ ______________________

REVIEW: CHAPTER 4 LESSONS 3–4

NAME ______________________

Review Word Families and Word Origins

Use the table to help you remember the meanings of the roots you learned.

Latin		Greek	
aud = hear	**aqua** = water	**chron** = time	**meter** = measure
vid, vis = see	**port** = carry	**bio** = life	**graph** = write
mar = sea	**rupt** = break	**cycl** = circle, ring	**scope** = see
ped = foot	**scrib, script** = write	**geo** = earth	**man** = hand
liber = free	**struct** = build	**phon** = sound	**ast** = star
ann, enn = year		**ology** = the study of	**therm** = heat

Match each word in column 1 to its definition in column 2. Write the letter of the definition on the line.

1. ______ anniversary

2. ______ manual

3. ______ synchronize

4. ______ geology

5. ______ portable

6. ______ centimeter

7. ______ rupture

8. ______ aquatic

9. ______ inscribe

10. ______ autobiography

11. ______ pedestrian

12. ______ audible

13. ______ submarine

14. ______ liberate

a. taking place in the water

b. moveable; able to be carried

c. the study of Earth

d. to write on or in something

e. a written account of a person's life

f. to let free

g. to break or burst

h. the day each year that marks a special event

i. able to be heard

j. a vehicle that travels under the water

k. to do something by hand

l. a measurement equal to 1/100 of a meter

m. to cause to happen at the same time

n. a person who is walking, or traveling by foot

NAME ____________________

Lesson 4.5 Pronunciation Key and Respellings

Next to each entry word in a dictionary, there is a **respelling** of the word. Special letters and symbols show how the word should be pronounced. A **pronunciation key** is a guide to using the letters and symbols found in respellings. It is usually found on every other page in a dictionary

Use the pronunciation key below to answer the questions in this lesson.

PRONUNCIATION KEY

/a/ = **a**t, t**a**p	/u/ = **u**p, c**u**t	/ə/ = a (**a**round, **a**bout)
/ā/ = **a**pe, s**ay**	/ū/ = **u**se, c**u**te	e (bett**e**r, tak**e**n)
/ä/ = f**a**r, h**ea**rt	/ü/ = r**u**le, c**oo**l	i (rabb**i**t, penc**i**l)
/â/ = c**a**re, h**ai**r	/u̇/ = p**u**ll, b**oo**k	o (doct**o**r, lem**o**n)
	/û/ = t**u**rn, v**e**rb	u (**u**pon, circ**u**s)
/e/ = **e**nd, g**e**t		
/ē/ = **e**ven, m**e**	/ch/ = **ch**in, tea**ch**	
/ê/ = pi**e**rce, f**ea**r		
	/ng/ = si**ng**, ha**ng**	
/i/ = **i**t, f**i**t		
/ī/ = **i**ce, t**ie**	/sh/ = **sh**op, ru**sh**	
/o/ = h**o**t, f**a**ther	/th/ = **th**in, bo**th**	
/ō/ = **o**ld, s**o**	/t͟h/ = **th**is, smoo**th**	
/ô/ = s**o**ng, b**ou**ght		
/ȯ/ = f**o**rk, c**o**rn	/hw/ = **wh**ite, **wh**y	
/oi/ = **oi**l, b**oy**		
/ou/ = **ou**t, h**ou**se	/zh/ = trea**su**re, bei**ge**	

Read the sentences below. Underline the words that the respellings in the box stand for.

/tom′ boi′/ /luv/ /bāst/ /sim′ ə lər/ /nov′ ə list/ /fik′ shən əl/
/stȯr′ ē/ /nōn/ /mem′ ə rēz/ /kâr′ ik tər/ /t͟hâr/

1. Louisa May Alcott was a novelist who was best known for her beloved children's book *Little Women.*
2. The book was partly based on memories of Louisa's own childhood.
3. There are four girls in the story, just as there were four Alcott girls.
4. In real life, Louisa was most similar to the character of Jo, a spunky tomboy with an active imagination.
5. Like the fictional Marches, the Alcotts were poor in money but rich in love and family.

NAME ___________________________

Lesson 4.5 Pronunciation Key and Respellings

Read each bold sound below. Use the pronunciation key to figure out its sound. Underline the word beside it that contains the same sound.

1. **/zh/**	zebraü	gigantic	pleasure
2. **/ü/**	plume	crumble	stunt
3. **/ə/**	gargoyle	pencil	poppy
4. **/ô/**	foot	shampoo	cause
5. **/ä/**	bizarre	plates	straighten
6. **/ē/**	enjoyable	oatmeal	omelet
7. **/th/**	weather	birthplace	sympathy

Read the sentences below. Rewrite each bold word using the letters and symbols in the pronunciation key. You do not need to worry about placing the accents, or stress marks.

1. The Cornhusker State is Nebraska's **nickname** ___________________.
2. The capital of Tennessee is Nashville, which is **located** ___________________ on the Cumberland River.
3. The bluebonnet has been the **official** ___________________ flower of Texas since 1901.
4. The Declaration of Independence was **signed** ___________________ in Philadelphia, Pennsylvania, in 1776.
5. Because Montana does not have a large **population** ___________________, it has only one U.S. representative.
6. The **chickadee** ___________________ is Maine's state bird.
7. Wisconsin has 93 state parks, forests, and recreation **areas** ___________________.
8. South Carolina was the first state to secede, or separate, from the United States during the **Civil** ___________________ War.

NAME ______________________________

Lesson 4.5 Pronunciation Key and Respellings

Read the following paragraphs. On the line that follows each bold word, rewrite the respelling.

Alaska is by far the /**lär′ gəst**/ __________________ of the 50 United States. In fact, if Alaska was a /**kun′ trē**/ __________________, it would be the 19th biggest nation in the world. Its /**pop yə lā′ shən**/ __________________, though, is the smallest of all the states, partly because Alaska is hard to /**rēch**/ __________________. It's about a 1,500-mile drive from Seattle, Washington, to Fairbanks, Alaska. Unlike /**en′ ē**/ __________________ other state, you have to travel through a /**fȯr′ in**/ __________________ country, Canada, to get there.

The first Europeans to settle this part of the world were /**rush′ əns**/ __________________ who hunted sea otters for their fur. In 1867, Secretary of State William Seward /**ûrjd**/ __________________ Congress to /**pûr′ chis**/ __________________ the Alaskan lands from Russia. /**ôl t͟hō′**/ __________________ the sale went through, it was very unpopular with American /**sit′ i zəns**/ __________________. They couldn't understand why our /**nā′ shən**/ __________________ needed to own such a cold, remote place.

Today, Alaska is one of the most /**bū′ tə fəl**/ __________________ areas of our nation. /**mil′ yəns**/ __________________ of /**ā′ kərs**/ __________________ are protected from development so wildlife can thrive without fear of human-made /**di struk′ shən**/ __________________. Tourism has become an important part of the Alaskan /**i kon′ ə mē**/ __________________. Other Alaskan /**in′ də strēs**/ __________________ include fishing, drilling for oil, mining coal, and the military.

NAME ______________________

Lesson 4.5 Pronunciation Key and Respellings

Use the pronunciation key on page 144 to answer the questions that follow.

1. Which symbol represents the long **o** sound, as in *colder*? ______________
2. Which two pairs of letters can make the **oi** sound, as in *soiled*? ______________
3. What are the key words for the /ê/ sound? ______________
4. Which symbol stands for the vowel sound you hear in *should*? ______________
5. What are the key words for the /ü/ sound? ______________
6. Which letters can make the /ə/ sound? ______________

Read each clue below and the respelling that follows. Say the respelling out loud to yourself. On the line, rewrite the word that matches the clue.

1. the sixth planet from the sun; known for its rings /sat′ ərn/ ______________
2. a person who works and travels in outer space /as′ trə not′/ ______________
3. to send a space vehicle forcefully into the air /lônch/ ______________
4. a rocky object that orbits the sun /as′ tə roid′/ ______________
5. a place where scientific experiments are done /lab′ rə tȯr′ ē/ ______________
6. the part of a space shuttle where a pilot sits /kôk′ pit/ ______________
7. an object that orbits another larger object /sa′ tə līt′/ ______________
8. the layer of gases that surround Earth /at′ mə sfêr′/ ______________
9. a space vehicle /spās′ kraft′/ ______________

Phonics Connection

Which two words in the second exercise have the same vowel sound as *crawl*?

______________ ______________

NAME ______________________________

Lesson 4.6 Accent Marks

An **accent mark** (′) tells which syllable of a word is stressed. The stressed syllable is said with more force.

- In *harness*, the first syllable is stressed: /här′ nis/. Try saying *harness* with the stress on the second syllable, and see if you can hear the difference.
- Some words have two accents. The **primary** accent is usually bold. The syllable with the **secondary** accent is said with less force.

  /pig′ tāl′/ /sev′ ən tĕnth′/ /sum′ bod′ ē/
- Remember, the schwa does not appear in stressed syllables.

Read each bold word out loud. Circle the letter of the respelling in which the primary accent mark is placed correctly.

	a.	b.
1. **violin**	a. /vī′ ə lin′/	b. /vī′ ə′ lin/
2. **trumpet**	a. /trum′ pit/	b. /trum pit′/
3. **cymbals**	a. /sim bəlz′/	b. /sim′ bəlz/
4. **tuba**	a. /tü′ bə/	b. /tü bə′/
5. **trombone**	a. /trôm′ bōn/	b. /trôm bōn′/
6. **cello**	a. /chel′ ō/	b. /chel ō′/
7. **clarinet**	a. /clâr′ ə′ net/	b. /clâr′ ə net′/
8. **piano**	a. /pī an′ ō/	b. /pī′ an ō/
9. **saxophone**	a. /sak′ sə fōn′/	b. /sak sə′ fōn′/

Read each respelling below out loud to yourself. Listen to which syllable is stressed and underline it. If you are not sure, try stressing different syllables.

1. /mū zish ən/
2. /in strə mənt/
3. /här mə nē/
4. /ôp ər ə/
5. /rith əm/
6. /kən duk tər/

NAME ______________________________

Lesson 4.6 Accent Marks

Read the paragraphs below. Add the primary accent to each bold respelling. If a word also contains a secondary accent, it has already been added for you.

The ukulele may not be the most /**pop yə lər**/ instrument, but as soon as most /**pē pəl**/ hear it, they love its /**plez ənt**/ sound. The Hawaiian ukulele, which looks like a small guitar, was modeled on a /**sim ə lər**/ Portuguese instrument brought to /**hə wī ē**/ in the 1870s. /**ôl thō**/ the ukulele had its /**grā test**/ /**pop′ yə lâr i tē**/ in the 1920s, it has /**rē sənt lē**/ been enjoying a new surge in /**in trist**/. One good /**rē zən**/ for this may be Jake Shimabukuro.

Jake was born and raised in Hawaii, where his /**muth ər**/ gave him his first ukulele lesson when he was /**ōn lē**/ four years old. He has great respect for traditional ukulele /**myū zik**/, but Jake also /**en joiz**/ showing the world just how much the ukulele can do. His music /**kən tānz**/ elements of many /**dif ər ənt**/ styles of music, /**in klü ding**/ jazz, /**blü gras′**/, classical, and rock. As he strums and plucks the ukulele, his fingers move so fast, they're hard to follow. He makes it /**ē zē**/ to /**un′ dər stand**/ why the name *ukulele* is Hawaiian for *jumping flea*!

Some multiple-meaning words are spelled the same but pronounced differently. For example, present can be pronounced /pri zent′/ or /prez′ ent/. The meaning changes depending on the pronunciation and on the stress. Read each sentence below. Circle the respelling that shows how the bold word is used in the sentence.

1. The winner of the **contest** will receive a new bike. /kôn′ test′/ /kən test′/
2. My dad found his favorite old **record** online. /rek′ ərd/ /ri kȯrd′/
3. *CD* is an acronym for ***compact*** *disk*. /kəm pakt′/ /kôm′ pakt/
4. Many plants are found only in the **desert**. /di zûrt′/ /dez′ ərt/

NAME ________________________

Review Respellings and Accent Marks

Read the paragraphs below. Underline the correct respelling of each bold word.

If you like spending time **outdoors** (/out dȯrz′/, /owt′ doors/) and are good at following **directions** (/dī rik′ shəns/, /di rek′ shənz/), you might like to **try** (/trē/, /trī/) your hand at geocaching. Geocaching is an **activity** (/ak tiv′ i tē/, /ack′ tiv ī te/) in which people follow directions to find a **small** (/smôl/, /smōl/) treasure, or cache (pronounced *cash*). Some people use a **special** (/spech′ āl/, /spesh′ əl/) device called a Global Positioning **System** (/sis′ təm/, /sis′ tēm/) (GPS), while others just use a **compass** (/cōm′ pēs/, /kum′ pəs/) and a map. There are more than 200,000 geocaches currently **hidden** (/hīd′ n/, /hid′ n/) in about 220 countries around the world. The coordinates, or longitude and latitude, to **these** (/thēz/, /t̲h̲ēz/) geocaches can be found online.

The hidden **treasure** (/treg′ ər/, /trezh′ ər/) is usually something small, like a toy, a **book** (/bu̇k/, /būk/) , a CD, or some unusual coins. **Many** (/men′ ē/, /män′ ē/) geocaches also include a logbook. **Each** (/ech/, /ēch/) person to find the cache can **record** (/rek′ ərd/, /ri kȯrd′/) his or her name and any **comments** (/kôm′ entz/, /kūm′ entz/) about finding the cache. If you **take** (/tak/, /tāk/) the cache, you must leave a new treasure in its place so that there will be **something** (/sum′ thing/, /süm′ thing/) for the next person to find. People like the thrill of seeking out something hidden and the **idea** (/i de′ ə/, /ī dē′ ə/ of connecting with **dozens** (/duz′ ənz/, /düz′ ēnz/) of other geocachers they **might** (/mīt/, /mite/) never actually meet. **Would** (/wūd/, /wu̇d/) you like to be a modern-day treasure hunter too?

Read each pair of words below. Say the words to yourself and circle the letter of the word that has the primary accent in the correct place.

1. **a.** /hə′ rī zən/ **b.** /hə rī′ zən/
2. **a.** /snē′ kər/ **b.** /snē kər′/
3. **a.** /səg jes′ chən/ **b.** /səg jes chən′/
4. **a.** /mō mənt′/ **b.** /mō′ mənt/
5. **a.** /hōp lis′/ **b.** /hōp′ lis/
6. **a.** /fər got′n/ **b.** /fər′ gotn/

NAME ___________________________

Review Respellings and Accent Marks

Read the instructions below. Rewrite each bold word using the letters and symbols in the pronunciation key. Include an accent to show which syllable is stressed. If you need help, you may use a dictionary.

Soda Boat

Materials:

- 2-liter plastic bottle
- **clay** __________________
- a straw
- $\frac{1}{4}$ cup **vinegar** __________________
- 1 tablespoon baking **soda** __________________
- paper towel

1. **Poke** __________________ a hole in the bottom of the bottle. **Insert** __________________ about $\frac{2}{3}$ of the straw into the hole. Make a seal **around** __________________ the straw using the clay.
2. Pour the vinegar into the bottle, making sure not to get any in the straw.
3. Tear off a **piece** __________________ of the paper towel, and place the baking soda on it. **Carefully** __________________ fold the towel around the baking soda, and twist both ends. This will **prevent** __________________ the vinegar from reaching the baking soda for a few **seconds** __________________.
4. Place the bottle in a tub of **water** __________________. The straw should be **beneath** __________________ the water so that it can act **like** __________________ a **motor** __________________.
5. Insert the paper towel and baking soda packet into the bottle, and twist on the bottle cap as **quickly** __________________ as you can.
6. **When** __________________ the baking soda and vinegar **react** __________________, they create **carbon** __________________ dioxide. It acts as gas and powers your "soda boat" across the water.

REVIEW: CHAPTER 4 LESSONS 5–6

Answer Key

page 6
1. cactus
2. gaze
3. grumble
4. geology
5. prince
6. orange
7. cube
8. fierce

1. juice
2. Georgia
3. goose
4. candle
5. gymnastics
6. glitter
7. cartwheel

page 7

<u>Hard **c**</u>	<u>Soft **c**</u>
called	ceremony
practitioner	place
include	society
culture	produced
basic	incense
rectangular	certain
cloth	
clean	
occasions	
can	
imperfections	

<u>Hard **g**</u>	<u>Soft **g**</u>
guests	age
removing	arranging
irregular	gestures
rectangular	fragile

page 8
hard **g**, soft **c**, hard **g**, hard **g**, soft **c**, hard **g**, hard **g**, soft **g**, hard **c**, hard **g**, hard **g**, soft **g**, hard **c**

1. called
2. England
3. decided
4. gathered, African

page 9

grapes	bridge
sugar	gypsy
griddle	oxygen
camera	celery
coupon	Iceland
computer	specific

1. Amelia spent the afternoon at her grandmother's house.
2. It was a cold and gloomy day, but the house was warm and cozy.
3. Granny Kay stirred a pot of gently simmering broth.
4. "Gumbo is a hot and spicy Louisiana soup or stew," said Granny Kay.
5. "White rice is one of the most important ingredients in gumbo."
6. "The secret is using the best shrimp, crab, and crawfish."
7. "It's also important to use plenty of fresh vegetable, like okra, tomatoes, bell peppers, onions, and celery."
8. Amelia tasted the gumbo from the wooden spoon. "Now I see why your recipe is so legendary in our family!" exclaimed Amelia.

page 10
1. s, z
2. s, z
3. z, z
4. z, z, s
5. s, s
6. z
7. z, s/z
8. zh, s, sh
9. zh/z, s

page 11
1. locksmith
2. cheese
3. pleasure
4. sure
5. tissue

1. spare
2. treasure
3. dries
4. cards
5. silence
6. listening
7. sugarcane

page 12
1. unusual
2. cellar
3. fragile
4. insurance
5. Georgia
6. government
7. picnic
8. tease
9. speechless
10. positive

n	k	e	t	y	m	m	f	t	n	g	u	a	a	e
m	l	o	e	r	n	p	v	c	y	s	n	q	w	c
j	i	f	r	a	g	i	l	e	g	t	u	c	i	o
l	p	s	p	e	e	c	h	l	e	s	s	v	n	a
q	f	t	o	b	o	n	d	l	e	x	u	h	s	p
t	e	a	s	e	r	i	b	a	r	v	a	f	u	l
n	k	f	i	r	g	c	b	r	z	e	l	g	r	y
j	u	w	t	p	i	g	q	w	a	p	o	g	a	t
n	u	r	i	t	a	n	w	e	u	u	k	l	n	d
h	g	o	v	e	r	n	m	e	n	t	e	r	c	v
j	y	b	e	d	s	r	t	k	c	l	s	n	e	p

page 13

<u>/s/ sound</u>	<u>/z/ sound</u>
clasped	pleasant
springtime	always
costly	wisdom
misplace	rosy

<u>/zh/ sound</u>	<u>/sh/ sound</u>
casual	sure
decision	sugar
measure	expansion
leisure	pressure

1. originally; soft **g**
2. peace; soft **c**
3. protect; hard **c**
4. large; soft **g**
5. underground; hard **g**
6. drawbridge; soft **g**

Answer Key

7. surrounding; hard **g**

page 14

Shelby; Chicago; Chris; chef; chic; choir; chose; shellfish; dish; Charlotte; chemist; She; research Charley; character; hunch; shy; such; Charley; champion; chess; chameleons; shaggy; sheepdog

/sh/ sound	/ch/ sound
Shelby	chose
Chicago	research
chef	Charley
chic	hunch
shellfish	such
dish	champion
Charlotte	chess
She	
shy	
shaggy	
sheepdog	

/k/ sound
Chris
choir
chemist
character
chameleons

page 15

1. b; th
2. c; wh
3. a; ph
4. a; th
5. c; wh
6. b; th

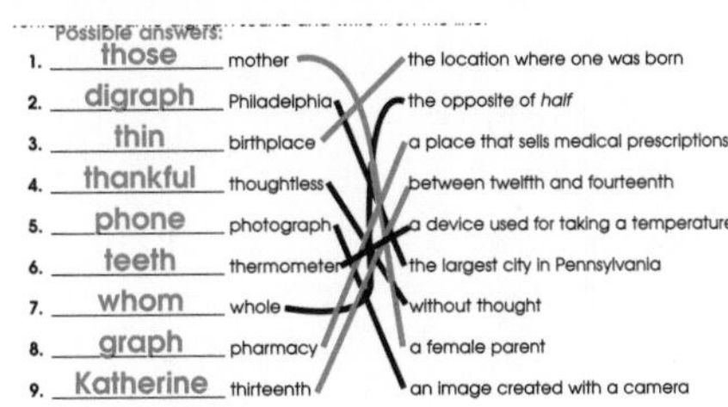
Possible answers:
1. those — mother — the location where one was born
2. digraph — Philadelphia — the opposite of *half*
3. thin — birthplace — a place that sells medical prescriptions
4. thankful — thoughtless — between twelfth and fourteenth
5. phone — photograph — a device used for taking a temperature
6. teeth — thermometer — the largest city in Pennsylvania
7. whom — whole — without thought
8. graph — pharmacy — a female parent
9. Katherine — thirteenth — an image created with a camera

page 16

ck, ng, ng, ng, ck, ck, gh, ng, ck, ck, gh, ng, ng, ng, ng, ng, ng, gh, ng, ck, ng, ck, ck, ck

page 17

1. Sitting on porches and sipping iced-tea is a neighborhood tradition on Ella's block.
2. On stormy summer evenings, when lightning streaks the sky, Ella and her brothers sit at the kitchen table and play cards.
3. Just thinking about summer makes Ella hungry for fresh strawberries.
4. She can't get enough of all the things that make up lazy summer days.
5. When the days get shorter and the nights get longer, Ella begins storing up her summer memories.

1. block; Possible answer: rock
2. wing; Possible answer: cling
3. clearing; Possible answer: fearing
4. tongue; Possible answer: rung
5. packet; Possible answer: jacket

page 18

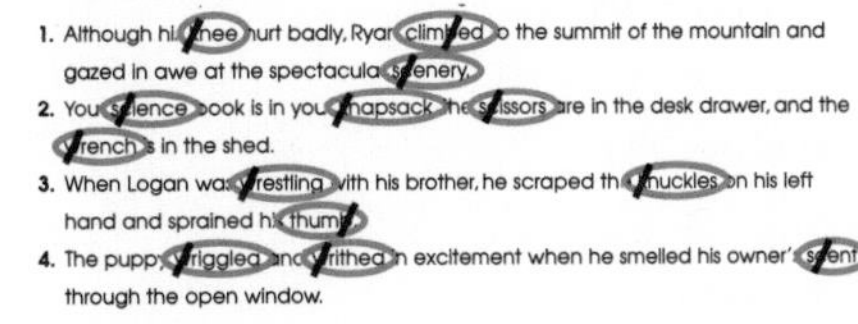
1. Although his knee hurt badly, Ryan climbed to the summit of the mountain and gazed in awe at the spectacular scenery.
2. Your science book is in your knapsack, the scissors are in the desk drawer, and the wrench is in the shed.
3. When Logan was wrestling with his brother, he scraped the knuckles on his left hand and sprained his thumb.
4. The puppy wriggled and writhed in excitement when he smelled his owner's scent through the open window.

1. knife
2. limb
3. thumb
4. wrap
5. knock

page 19

1. kn; b
2. wr; c
3. mb; a
4. wr; b
5. kn; a
6. wr; b
7. mb; b

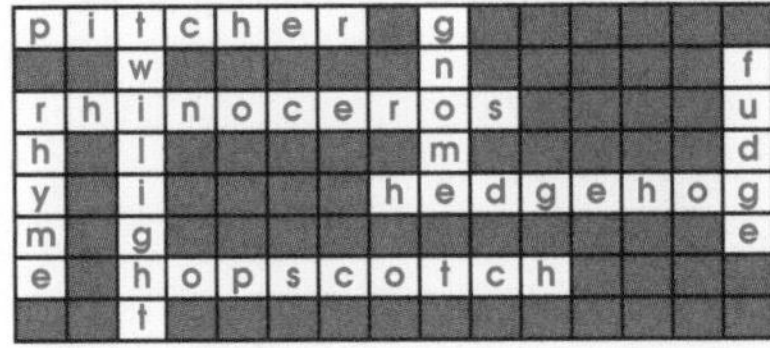
1. Marie Curie was a scientist who was known for her work with radiation.
2. If you wring out the wet towels before you hang them on the clothesline, they will dry much more quickly.
3. Rosie and Daniel helped paint the scenery for the play.
4. The robin hungrily watched the fat worm wriggling out of its hole.
5. In the famous nursery rhyme, Little Jack Horner put his thumb into a pie and pulled out a plum.
6. Use a pair of scissors to cut out the article in the newspaper.
7. Grandma made a wreath to hang on the front door.
8. You must knead the bread dough and then let it rise for an hour.

page 20

p	i	t	c	h	e	r		g						
		w						n						f
r	h	i	n	o	c	e	r	o	s					u
h		l						m						d
y		i					h	e	d	g	e	h	o	g
m		g												e
e		h	o	p	s	c	o	t	c	h				
		t												

page 21

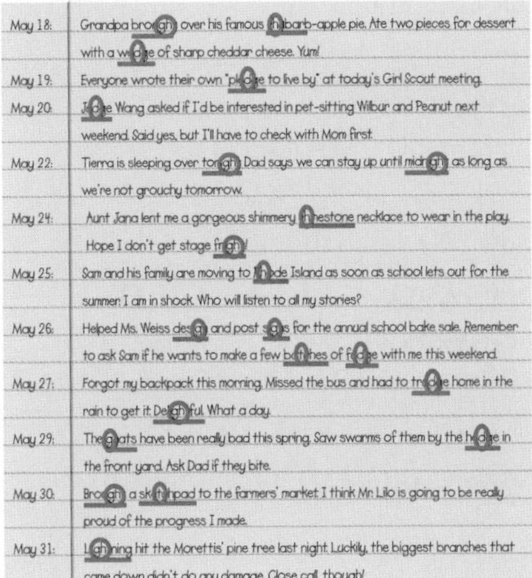
May 18:	Grandpa brought over his famous rhubarb-apple pie. Ate two pieces for dessert with a wedge of sharp cheddar cheese. Yum!
May 19:	Everyone wrote their own "pledge to live by" at today's Girl Scout meeting.
May 20:	Judge Wang asked if I'd be interested in pet-sitting Wilbur and Peanut next weekend. Said yes, but I'll have to check with Mom first.
May 22:	Tierra is sleeping over tonight. Dad says we can stay up until midnight as long as we're not grouchy tomorrow.
May 24:	Aunt Jana lent me a gorgeous shimmery rhinestone necklace to wear in the play. Hope I don't get stage fright!
May 25:	Sam and his family are moving to Rhode Island as soon as school lets out for the summer. I am in shock. Who will listen to all my stories?
May 26:	Helped Ms. Weiss design and post signs for the annual school bake sale. Remember to ask Sam if he wants to make a few batches of fudge with me this weekend.
May 27:	Forgot my backpack this morning. Missed the bus and had to trudge home in the rain to get it. Delightful. What a day.
May 29:	The gnats have been really bad this spring. Saw swarms of them by the hedge in the front yard. Ask Dad if they bite.
May 30:	Brought a sketchpad to the farmers' market. I think Mr. Lilo is going to be really proud of the progress I made.
May 31:	Lightning hit the Morettis' pine tree last night. Luckily, the biggest branches that came down didn't do any damage. Close call, though!

page 22

1. ci
2. ti, ti

3. ci
4. ci, ti
5. ti
6. ti
7. ti
8. ti, ti
9. ti, ci
10. ti, ci, ci, ci

page 23
1. d
2. e
3. b
4. f
5. g
6. h
7. i
8. c
9. a

1. magician
2. Addition, subtraction, multiplication
3. Egyptian, ancient
4. electrician
5. Martians
6. official

page 24
Ch, /ch/ sound; ng, /ng/ sound; ng, /ng/ sound; ck, /k/ sound; th, /th/ sound; ch, /ch/ sound; ng, /ng/ sound; sh, /sh/ sound; th, /th/ sound; Wh, /hw/ sound; th, /th/ sound; ck, /k/ sound; ng, /ng/ sound

page 25

1. roam	gnome	7. fine	sign
2. some	thumb	8. dodge	lodge
3. college	knowledge	9. teeth	wreath
4. which	stitch	10. green	scene
5. grime	rhyme	11. buckle	knuckle
6. sly	thigh	12. kissed	wrist

1. magician
2. dictionary
3. directions
4. eruption
5. artificial
6. special
7. definition
8. commercial
9. delicious
10. fraction

page 26

1. hard icy pellets that fall from the sky	hail
2. a homophone for *rains*	reins
3. a Scandinavian country bordered by Sweden and Finland	Norway
4. a vehicle pulled by horses over snow	sleigh
5. to do what one is told to do	obey

mermaid; waist; tail; entertains; today; may; plays; always; they; remain; neighbors

page 27
1. Braille
2. Aids
3. played
4. waist
5. may
6. main
7. weighed
8. they
9. Crayons
10. Dayton
11. conveyer

page 28
1. b, c, d
2. a, b, c
3. a, c, d
4. b, d
5. a, c, d

chimney shield
medley hairpiece
attorney relief

sheep peach
sneezing squeal
succeed sunbeam

1. movie
2. windshield
3. nominee
4. sneak

page 29
ea, ee, ey, ey, ie, ee, ea, ea, ee, ea, ee, ea, ie, ee, ea, ea, ee, ee

page 30
1. valentine
2. impolite
3. copyright
4. provide
5. hind
6. combine
7. unwind
8. eyesight
9. blind

page 31
1. h
2. d
3. c
4. i
5. b
6. a
7. f
8. g
9. e

Answer Key

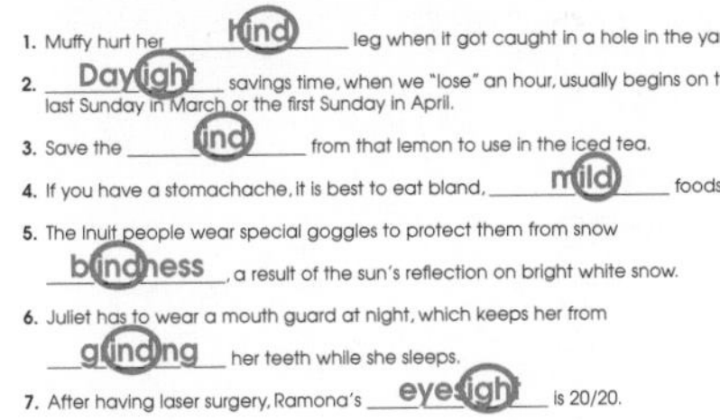

1. Muffy hurt her hind leg when it got caught in a hole in the yard.
2. Daylight savings time, when we "lose" an hour, usually begins on the last Sunday in March or the first Sunday in April.
3. Save the rind from that lemon to use in the iced tea.
4. If you have a stomachache, it is best to eat bland, mild foods.
5. The Inuit people wear special goggles to protect them from snow blindness, a result of the sun's reflection on bright white snow.
6. Juliet has to wear a mouth guard at night, which keeps her from grinding her teeth while she sleeps.
7. After having laser surgery, Ramona's eyesight is 20/20.

page 32
moaned; groaned; grown; petticoats; below; cold; almost; most; cloak; flow; gold; broach; stroll

page 33
1. raincoat
2. poll
3. coast
4. billfold
5. crow
6. stagecoach
7. scold
8. charcoal
9. outgrow
10. rowboat

s	c	o	l	d	g	e	p	o	l	l	w	v	n	i
j	t	m	c	v	a	r	r	n	p	m	o	f	d	c
o	b	l	n	s	t	a	g	e	c	o	a	c	h	b
u	t	d	q	m	o	i	b	s	j	x	q	h	i	l
t	h	r	e	y	o	n	n	m	w	t	e	a	y	c
g	d	f	r	t	h	c	q	z	b	y	c	r	o	w
r	b	i	l	l	f	o	l	d	g	t	r	c	n	p
o	o	n	b	g	e	a	w	r	n	s	k	o	l	p
w	i	b	l	l	v	t	t	y	d	c	o	a	s	t
h	a	o	b	n	r	o	w	b	o	a	t	l	v	i

page 34
ost, ey, ea, ee, ai, old, igh, ea, ay, ay, old, ey, ow, ai

page 35
long **a**, long **e**, long **e**, long **a**, long **e**, long **e**, long **e**, long **o**, long **a**, long **a**, long **e**, long **e**, long **a**, long **e**, long **o**, long **i**, long **e**, long **o**, long **e**, long **e**, long **o**, long **i**, long **o**, long **a**, long **i**, long **o**, long **e**

page 36
1. ui
2. oo
3. ui
4. oo
5. oo
6. ou
7. ui
8. ew
9. ui

1. neighborhood
2. scrapbook
3. soup
4. tooth
5. new

page 37
1. a
2. b
3. b
4. c

Cameron: I appreciate that you agreed to do this interview. I'm very interested to hear your point of view on your job and being an artist today.

Mr. Hopper: I'm happy to speak with you about my work. I think your interest in art is very cool.

C: What was your childhood like? When did you first know that you wanted to create cartoon characters?

MH: I always knew I wanted to be an artist. I wasn't sure what kind until I finished high school and a friend introduced me to some great cartoons.

C: How did you ever come up with a kangaroo who plays the kazoo or a tattooed baboon named Lou who dreams of traveling to the moon?

MH: I guess my characters seem pretty wacky. Ideas come easily to me, so I have to sift through them to find the ones that are suitable for a particular cartoon. Fatherhood has also been an inspiration. If I can create something my kids think is a hoot, there's a good chance other kids will like it too.

C: I'm so glad you took the time to talk with me. Any last words of advice?

MH: Art isn't an easy way to make your livelihood, but there is nothing that would be more satisfying for me. Best of luck in all your pursuits.

page 38
audio
launch
malt
crawl
talking
salt
drawn
daughter
faucet
birdcall

page 39
1. Australia
2. smallest
3. called
4. awfully
5. Because, fauna
6. claws
7. rainfall

1. b
2. e
3. h
4. f
5. a
6. d
7. c
8. g

page 40
boycott; exploiting; employees; joining; voice; avoid; loyalty; disappoint; point; rejoiced

<u>/oy/ as in *destroy*</u>
boycott
employees
loyalty

<u>/oy/ as in *ointment*</u>
exploiting
joining
voice
avoid
disappoint
point
rejoiced

Answer Key

page 41

The word *Chinatown* refers to a section of a city that has a large number of Chinese people and businesses even though the city itself is not Chinese. Today, Chinatowns can be found all around the world. In North America, many were formed in the 1800s when the Chinese faced much discrimination. Luckily, things are different nowadays, and Chinatowns are seen as interesting places to visit—full of local culture, foods, and other goods.

Chinatowns are often located in urban settings, near the downtown areas of large cities. A large red arch with Chinese characters often marks the entrance to Chinatown. In the past, the arches were gifts from China, but today many are built locally. Street signs in Chinatown are often bilingual, or written in more than one language. Most Chinatowns abound with restaurants. Some serve authentic Chinese dishes. Others are visited by tourists and serve dishes like chop suey or chow mein.

Since some business owners still have strong ties to China, there are many stores that sell Chinese goods. For example, they carry loud Chinese firecrackers for the New Year celebration and colorful paper lanterns. The markets sell large amounts of Asian foods that may be difficult to find elsewhere. In Chinatown, it is easy to pick up some seaweed, black duck eggs, oyster sauce, and countless types of fowl.

If you have the chance, it's worth taking the time to prowl the streets of a Chinatown near you. The sights and sounds are sure to astound you.

page 42

				s	i	d	e	w	a	l	k	
		d		u								
		a		i								
		w	a	t	e	r	f	a	l	l		
		n		c		o		u				
				a		o		c				
				s		t		t	h	r	e	w
c	a	s	h	e	w			i				
								o				
		r	a	c	c	o	o	n				

page 43

1. oy
2. ou
3. oi
4. ow
5. oi
6. ou
7. ow

1. Scouts; campground
2. noise
3. appointed
4. boys; about; without
5. cookout; sirloin; moist; brownies

page 44

1. major
2. pyramids
3. tomatoes
4. recipe
5. barrel
6. severe
7. aware
8. dinosaur
9. pandas

1. gather
2. humor
3. oxygen
4. loyal
5. amount
6. coconut

page 45

system; visitor; solar; Normally; powerful; away; Horizons; Jupiter; giant; summer; discover

totem; e dragon; o
pasta; a pencil; i

page 46

peddəl; grumbəld; pebbəl; drizzəl; purpəl; troubəl; wrinkəld; cackəl; beagəl; nibbəl; twinkəl

page 47

1. Bernarr Macfadden was known as the "**Fa·ther** of Physical Culture."
2. In 1903, he founded the Coney Island **Po·lar** Bear Club.
3. **Mem·bers** of the club go swimming in the ocean during the **win·ter**.
4. Macfadden believed that the cold **wa·ter** was good for one's health.
5. The Coney **Is·land** Club isn't the only group of **ba·thers** who like the shock of taking a dip in frigid temperatures.
6. People all **a·round** the country share a passion for this unusual habit.
7. **To·day**, the members of the Coney Island Club swim every Sunday from October through **A·pril**.
8. Early in the **sea·son**, the temperature is in the low 60s, but later in the winter, it drops to **a·bout** 33 degrees.
9. The **swim·mers** wear nothing but regular bathing suits and surf boots to protect their feet.
10. On New Year's Day 2005, they raised money for the **Spe·cial** Olympics.
11. More than **se·ven** hundred swimmers headed for the icy Atlantic that day.
12. There is **e·ven** a movie about the Polar Bear Club and Coney Island in winter called *Side Shows by the Sea Shore*.

page 48

/y/, as in *yam*
yogurt
yak
yowling

long **i**, as in *try*
python
sky
analyze

short **i**, as in *gym*
physical
Egypt
typical

long **e**, as in *city*
celery
jellyfish
story

1. gym
2. hyenas
3. carry
4. mystery
5. rhyme
6. supply
7. style
8. myth

page 49

long **i** spelled **y**: try, buy, supply

long **e** spelled **y**: very, probably, creamy, immediately, approximately, tightly, gently, finally, ready, yummy, honey, strawberry

short **i** spelled **y**: mysterious, typical

/y/ spelled **y**: yogurt, you, yet, your, yummy

page 50

1. person
2. particular
3. border
4. birth

Answer Key

5. sworn
6. farther
7. squirrel
8. alarm
9.support

1. preserve
2. lifeguard
3. ignore
4. disturb
5. backyard
6. acorn

page 51
discover; Pitcher; person; however; water; thirsty; soldiers; operates; injured; over; remainder; Later; honors; her; officer; During; consider; earlier; After; worked; other; veterans; merged; together

page 52
1. eer
2. are
3. air
4. ear
5. are
6. eer
7. ear
8. ear
9. air
10. ear

1. volunteer
2. nightmare
3. gear
4. upstairs
5. reappear
6. seared

page 53
spear; welfare; pear; affair; bear; pair; reindeer; sneer; swearing; steer; deer; disappear; square; flare; stare; airplane

page 54
1. seven
2. America
3. stumble
4. circus
5. sculptor
6. ruffle

1. impolite
2. liberty
3. Egyptian
4. oval
5. welcome
6. maroon
7. grumble
8. adore
9. open
10. maple

page 55
1. nylon
2. yield
3. system
4. yo-yo
5. suddenly

1. picture; worth; words
2. turn; deserves; another
3. fair
4. Short
5. quitter; never; winner; never
6. unturned
7. Appearances
8. darkest; before
9. acorns
10. bird; worth
11. doctor
12. Misery

page 56
excite; read; discover; write; tell; live; marry; love; get; hope; choose; run; listen; dance; begin

page 57
travel; calls; fetches; supplies; tosses; catches; amplifies; keeps; buzz; relaxes; watches; terrifies; pretends

page 58
1. tall
2. heavy
3. old
4. big
5. sunny
6. rich
7. windy
8. smelly
9. high

page 59
1. more interesting
2. most dangerous
3. rarest
4. shallower
5. dimmer
6. most unusual

1. Answers will vary.
2. Answers will vary.

circle *strange* and *dangerous*; underline *big*

Answer Key

page 60

1. crunch
2. prepare
3. bury
4. polish
5. regret
6. perceive
7. coax
8. petrify
9. deny
10. reduce
11. scurry
12. laugh

1. dreams
2. guesses
3. stands; cries
4. amplifies
5. hurries; searches
6. tosses
7. beats; relaxes
8. tries; leaves; soars
9. buzzes; wakes

page 61

1. escaped; Answers will vary.
2. grinning; Answers will vary.
3. emptying; Answers will vary.
4. freezing; Answers will vary.
5. worried; Answers will vary.

Base Word	"More"	"Most"
careful	more careful	most careful
sticky	stickier	stickiest
close	closer	closest
thin	thinner	thinnest
sleepy	sleepier	sleepiest
popular	more popular	most popular
sad	sadder	saddest
early	earlier	earliest
valuable	more valuable	most valuable
safe	safer	safest

page 62

1. foxes
2. scarves
3. popsicles
4. libraries
5. sandwiches
6. hooves
7. diaries

h	p	g	t	j	i	q	m	v	h	o	o	v	e	s
f	o	x	e	s	s	s	k	l	q	k	p	b	v	c
r	p	g	u	w	v	s	o	p	n	e	b	e	r	a
h	s	a	n	d	w	i	c	h	e	s	r	t	t	r
d	i	a	r	i	e	s	g	h	a	n	m	e	o	v
h	c	y	w	j	n	c	j	a	u	i	r	p	g	e
j	l	i	b	r	a	r	i	e	s	t	y	g	b	s
h	e	j	p	e	e	s	s	b	n	d	r	l	t	m
h	s	r	b	d	j	u	h	p	o	r	v	e	s	r

page 63

1. potato
2. mangoes
3. pistachios
4. rodeos
5. flamingos

1. Heroes
2. Kangaroos
3. Shampoos
4. Tomatoes

kangaroos; shampoos

page 64

1. oxen
2. sheep
3. moose
4. goose
5. salmon
6. deer

1. three mice
2. three dice
3. four teeth
4. four men
5. four feet

page 65

1. children; child
2. geese; goose
3. mice; mouse
4. foot; feet
5. die; dice
6. tooth; teeth

1. series
2. feet
3. ✓
4. ✓

child; mice; die; dice

page 66

SP; SP; SP; SP; PL; SP; PP; PL; PL; SP; PL

page 67

1. Winnie Foster is the main character in Natalie Babbit's book *Tuck Everlasting*.
2. The book *Cowboys and Longhorns* tells about the cowboys' struggle to run longhorn cattle from Texas to Kansas.
3. There are many amazing photographs in the nonfiction book *Volcanoes: Journey to the Crater's Edge*.
4. *The Watsons Go to Birmingham—1963* by Christopher Paul Curtis tells about the Watsons' experiences as they travel south one summer.
5. In *Holes* by Louis Sachar, Stanley Yelnats figures out how to change his family's bad luck.
6. *Millicent Min, Girl Genius* is about an 11-year-old girl's life and how she copes with the challenges of growing up.
7. Kevin Henkes's book *Olive's Ocean* was published in 2003.
8. Gary Paulsen has written four books about the same character, but I like *Brian's Winter* best.
9. *There's a Boy in the Girls' Bathroom* is my favorite Louis Sachar novel.
10. Karen Cushman has written several historical novels, like *The Midwife's Apprentice*.
11. Ruby Bridges's story of integrating an all-white elementary school in 1960 is told in *Through My Eyes*.
12. *The Penderwicks: A Summer Tale of Four Sisters, Two Rabbits, and a Very Interesting Boy* won the National Book Award for Young People's Literature.
13. In *Esperanza Rising* Esperanza's life changes when she must move to California and live at a migrant farm workers' camp.

page 68

1. geese
2. buffaloes
3. lions
4. finches
5. mosquitoes
6. wolves
7. oxen
8. foxes
9. rhinos

Answer Key

10. trout

Singular	Plural	Singular Possessive	Plural Possessive
pastry	pastries	pastry's	pastries'
auto	autos	auto's	autos'
grass	grasses	grass's	grasses'
enemy	enemies	enemy's	enemies'
mouse	mice	mouse's	mice's
portfolio	portfolios	portfolio's	portfolios'
branch	branches	branch's	branches'

1. rhinos
2. Possible answer: lions, swarm

page 69

sister's; teacher's; class's Watts'; Erin's; doors'; movies'

1. the violin belonging to my sister
2. the name of my teacher
3. the first recital of my class
4. the house belonging to the Watts
5. the bedroom belonging to Erin
6. the hinges of the doors
7. the plots of the movies

page 70

1. mouse/trap
2. rose/bud
3. thunder/storm
4. lawn/mower
5. high / school
6. apple/sauce

Possible answers: everybody, everything, everywhere, everyone, handbook, handmade, handshake, handstand, downhill, downstairs, downtown, seafood, seashore, seaweed, seashell, raincoat, raindrop, rainbow

lawn; sauce

page 71

grandparents; weekend; outside; doorstep; handshake; eyeglasses; woodworker; dining room; bedrooms; birdhouses; handmade; cookbooks; beehives; beekeeping; roadside; storyteller; Without; sunset; popcorn; snowstorms; notebook; classroom; something; bookcase; grandfather; lifetime

page 72

Word +	Word =	Contraction
would	have	would've
they	will	they'll
are	not	aren't
I	have	I've
let	us	let's
there	would	there'd
he	is	he's
does	not	doesn't
we	are	we're

1. doesn't
2. there's
3. she'd

page 73

you've; you'll; aren't; It'd; meal's; isn't; he'll; mustn't; shouldn't; That'll; might've; it's; hadn't; Don't; They'd;

you have
are not
meal is
he will
should not
might have
had not
they would

you will
it would
is not
must not
that will
it is
do not

page 74

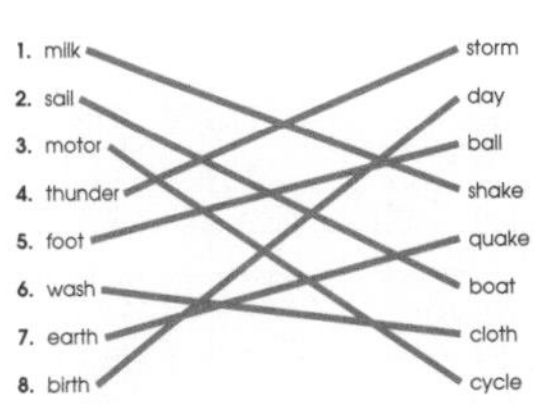

milkshake
sailboat
motorcycle
thunderstorm
football
washcloth
earthquake
birthday

1. handbook
2. sawdust
3. starfish
4. sunflower
5. tablespoon
6. horseback

motor; thunder; earth; birth; storm

page 75

1. wasn't
2. might've
3. haven't; you'll
4. That's
5. he'd
6. It's
7. he's; that've
8. There's
9. you're

Possible answers: styles; variety; you

page 76

1. unseen; seen
2. unequal; equal
3. nonspecific; specific
4. unfamiliar; familiar
5. nonathletic; athletic

Answer Key

uncomfortable; unsteady;
uncertainly; disobey;
unsure; disbelief
disqualified; unwelcome;
nonstop; uneasy;
disappointed

					c													
					o						c							
					w						o							
					o				c	o	e	x	i	s	t	i	n	g
m	i	d	t	e	r	m					d							
					k						u							
			i		e						c							
		i	m	p	r	a	c	t	i	c	a	l						
			m		s						t							
			a								i							
			t					i	n	c	o	r	r	e	c	t		
			u								n							
			r															
			e															

page 77

page 78
1. postelection
2. preordered
3. misunderstood
4. rechecked
5. misheard
6. retraced
7. misread
8. restate
9. preview

page 79
1. uniforms
2. trilingual
3. multivitamin
4. trilogy
5. triceratops
6. Multicultural
7. bifocals
8. tricolor
9. bicentennial
10. tristate
11. unicycle

page 80
1. overuse
2. underdone
3. undercharge
4. oversized
5. undercook

1. superfine
2. subzero
3. superabsorbent
4. subaquatic
5. supersensitive

page 81

1. e	**a.** anti
2. g	**b.** anti
3. a	**c.** semi
4. f	**d.** en
5. c	**e.** semi
6. d	**f.** en
7. b	**g.** semi

1. semidarkness
2. semisweet
3. ensuring
4. engulfed
5. antitheft
6. encouraged

page 82
passion; decision;
appreciation; fascination;
completion; devotion;
determination;
communication;
identification; attraction;
mission

Answers will vary.

page 83
1. safety
2. exchangeable
3. generosity
4. humidity
5. allowable

1. impossible
2. loyalty, honesty
3. memorable
4. irresistible
5. ability

1. loyalty
2. almost; most

(page 84)
1. sympathetic
2. sharpen
3. romantic
4. enthusiastic
5. lighten
6. deepen
7. optimistic

1. woven
2. specific; historic
3. straighten
4. strategic
5. broaden

(page 85)
awareness; assistance;
craftsmanship;
circumstances; darkness;
persistence; quickness;
independence;
performance; fondness;
endurance; hardships

Answers will vary.

(page 86)
1. greenish
2. guitarist
3. British

4. specialist
5. racist
6. stylish

1. pharmacist
2. artist
3. dentist
4. novelist
5. geologist
6. florist

page 87
1. thirst/i/ness
2. natural/ly; artificial/ly
3. tradition/al/ly
4. historic/al/ly
5. flexibil/ity
6. thought/ful/ness

1. Answers will vary.
2. Answers will vary.

1. long e
2. Possible answers: trying, gymnast

page 88
- recycle
- unable, reuse
- inexpensive
- ensure
- overcrowded
- biweekly
- antipollution

page 89
1. fragrance
2. foolish
3. noticeable
4. straighten
5. happiness
6. enthusiastic
7. generosity

8. congratulation
9. biologist
10. reversible
11. citizenship
12. violinist
13. magnetic
14. intelligence

page 90

umbrella; 3 boots; 1
pretzel; 2 caterpillar; 4

tornado; 3 pumpkin; 2

umbrellə; pretzəl; catərpillər

page 91
Ken/nel; trav/el; year/ly; Gar/den; most/ly; sport/ing; To/day; tal/ents; work/ing; show/case; Win/ners; com/pete; ti/tle; herd/ing; ca/nines; O/ver; sheep/dogs; bull/dogs; al/most; ho/nor
rare/ly; ev/er; sec/ond; mon/ey; breed/ing; fu/ture

page 92
par. 1: 2, 3, 1, 2, 3, 2, 3, 2, 2, 1, 1
par. 2: 2, 3, 2, 2, 1, 3, 2, 2, 3, 2, 3, 3, 1, 2, 2, 1
par. 3: 2, 2, 2, 1, 3, 3, 3, 2, 4
par. 4: 2, 3, 2, 3, 3

page 93
1. foot/step; service
2. club; birds
3. in/ven/tion; magical
4. wa/ter/mel/on; adorable
5. book/case; effort

1. Coretta Scott King was known as the wife of Martin Luther King but also as a civil rights activist herself.
2. She met her husband at the New England Conservatory.
3. Coretta's Freedom Concerts used both poetry and music to communicate with people and bring their attention to the issues she cared about.
4. Coretta opposed the Vietnam War and organized people in protest.
5. After her husband's death in 1968, Coretta worked to keep his memory and his dreams of peace and racial equality alive.
6. Coretta also worked to end racial segregation in South Africa.
7. The Coretta Scott King Book Award is given to outstanding African American authors and illustrators of children's books.

1. invention; vacation
2. sighed

page 94
1. a
2. b
3. b
4. c
5. a

1. inaccurate
2. foreign
3. safety
4. dull
5. male's
6. repel
7. different

page 95
1. S
2. A
3. A
4. S
5. S
6. A
7. S
8. S

Answers will vary. Possible answers:
1. Most of the birds in this area fly south for the winter.
2. I awoke to a amazing sunrise this morning.
3. A fever is a common symptom of the flu.

Answer Key

4. When Samantha's goldfish died, she buried it under a tree in the yard.
5. Mrs. Schmidt said that the drawing was done by an unknown artist.
6. Makenna's basement flooded during the heavy rains in April.
7. The sky turned deep purple as a severe storm approached the city.

page 96

while; few; problem; destroy; supply; occupations; ended; private; imaginative; smallest; unemployed; totally; assist; useless

page 97

1. together
2. liberty
3. consume
4. cautious
5. straight
6. locate
7. appear
8. present
9. annoy
10. reply

t	c	u	p	e	g	g	y	t	e	b	s	l	k	f
h	a	p	p	e	a	r	n	l	o	c	a	t	e	n
j	u	h	y	y	w	n	a	i	h	o	p	h	v	s
f	t	b	p	s	g	m	u	b	q	n	g	d	z	n
o	i	o	r	r	w	f	q	e	h	s	v	q	f	l
t	o	g	e	t	h	e	r	r	d	u	e	p	m	r
v	u	c	s	j	u	f	k	t	a	m	z	k	g	e
r	s	a	e	t	t	p	b	y	n	e	o	p	e	p
r	a	n	n	o	y	e	a	v	b	f	l	p	r	l
g	t	c	t	u	b	h	a	d	s	l	j	u	i	y
k	t	a	y	e	x	s	t	r	a	i	g	h	t	n

page 98

1. developed; grew
2. naughty; bad
3. seal; close
4. thawed; melted
5. ensnared; caught

1. edge; Possible answer: We crossed the border between Ohio and Indiana on our way to Chicago, Illinois.
2. rest; Possible answer: Relax and enjoy the movie.
3. fresh; Possible answer: My new shoes gave me a blister on my right foot.

page 99

active; lies; allowed; surface; habitat; creatures; total; returned; machines; survives; tiny

page 100

1. brownie
2. piano
3. algebra
4. rage
5. sneakers

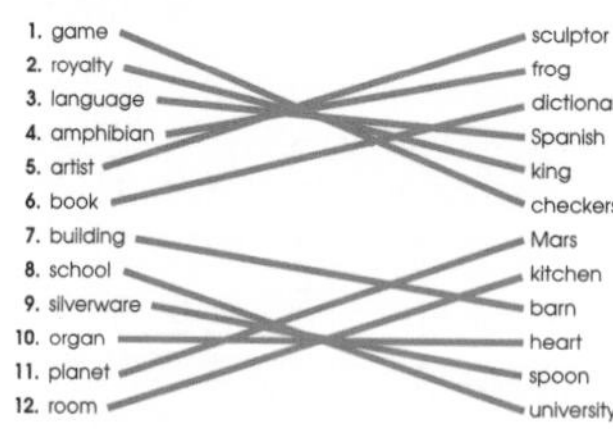

page 101

1. broccoli
2. basketball
3. lemonade
4. blizzard
5. Iguanodon
6. brother
7. boats
8. evergreens
9. watercolor

sibling, painting

page 102

1. images
2. easy
3. study
4. ancient
5. experts
6. influenced
7. region
8. found
9. noticed
10. interesting

page 103

1. discovered; detected
2. vacant; empty
3. heal; cure
4. aid; help

1. German
2. Plaid
3. soprano
4. fabric
5. fossil
6. symbol
7. Loneliness
8. birthday
9. finger

page 104

Aunt
Eight; real; your; meat; cereals
Plain
Choose
Chili
carrots; our
brewed; tea

desserts; made; piece; two

page 105

1. meddle	medal
2. knight	night
3. sun	son
4. sail	sale
5. stair	stare
6. fair	fare
7. lesson	lessen
8. heal	heel
9. herd	heard

page 106
Answers will vary. Possible answers are shown.
1. Maria deposited $25 in her bank account.
2. The evening train is bound for Baltimore.
3. The bronco bucked and tried to toss its rider to the ground.
4. I can't swallow my vitamin without having something to drink.
5. Eduardo likes his burgers rare, but I like mine well done.
6. Mom taught me how to change a tire last weekend.

1. river
2. hear

page 107
b; a; a; b; b; a; b; a; b

page 108
been; might; our; be; to; made; steel; Do; know; its; by; choose; would; their; peak; chance; see

page 109
1. Did you clip the leash to the collar?
2. The fair maiden kissed the prince.
3. Carlos is in a soccer league.
4. The detective is in grave danger.
5. The rash is from poison ivy.
6. The lemonade is too tart.
7. Where is Libby's tennis racket?
8. The boat is in the bay.
9. Cara bought three yards of fabric.

page 110
graduate; taxicab; airplane; dormitory; laboratories; hamburgers; bicycle; advertisement; veterinarian; statistics

page 111
1. CIA
2. NASA
3. UFO
4. MIA

1. FYI	by the way
2. LOL	in my opinion
3. TIA	as soon as possible
4. BTW	thanks in advance
5. ASAP	for your information
6. IMO	laughing out loud

(Lines connect: 1. FYI – for your information; 2. LOL – laughing out loud; 3. TIA – thanks in advance; 4. BTW – by the way; 5. ASAP – as soon as possible; 6. IMO – in my opinion)

page 112
1. war
2. Anne
3. like
4. not
5. memos
6. won
7. hid
8. stinky
9. Don't
10. frost
11. Adam
12. dine
13. mayor
14. Dr.
15. am
16. odd

page 113
travelogue; humongous; brash; splurge; mopeds; glimmer; brunch; slathered; smog; Internet; flurry

page 114
1. ad
2. fridge; burgers
3. zoo
4. mini; lab
5. bike
6. teens
7. photo

1. GPA
2. VIP
3. IRS
4. AKA
5. ATM
6. SCUBA

page 115

1. ✓ A man, a plan, a canal, Panama!	____ Red roots are put up to order.
2. ____ Sages can use gas.	✓ We'll let Dad tell Lew.
3. ____ No lemon, and no melon.	✓ Wontons? Not now.
4. ✓ Della sailed, Eva waved, Elias ailed.	____ Pals can slap.
5. ____ Was it Elliot's toilets I saw?	✓ Race fast, safe car.

1. sting
2. infomercial
3. camera

4. poodle
5. boom
6. crunch
7. sportscast
8. Muppet

Answers will vary.

1. sages
2. race

page 116

1. Once the storm had passed, the sea was as smooth as glass.
2. In the sun, Maureen's hair was as bright and shiny as a new copper penny.
3. After staying up so late the night before, Bailey moved as slowly as a snail on Saturday morning.
4. The secret was like a heavy weight that Damian carried on his shoulders.
5. When the water had boiled, the teakettle whistled like a cheerful bird on a spring morning.
6. Lola's heart dropped like a stone as she watched her father read her report card.

1. bits of confetti; multicolored snowflakes
2. Amanda's hair; curly as a poodle's
3. Julio; a turtle
4. cacti; soldiers
5. legs; tree trunks
6. hawk; kite
7. grandmother; kitten

page 117

the smell of freshly baked muffins danced through Meena's bedroom; the moon, a thin silvery smile; A soothing hand on her forehead was a cool towel; The sari she wore was a puddle of brilliant blue; The sun was a spotlight; Listening to you recite Shakespeare is music to my ears; You're going to be a hit

page 118

Answers will vary. Possible answers:

1. a caravan of camels
2. fingers
3. fingernails on a chalkboard
4. a dozen tiny hammers pounding on my head
5. stars dotting the night sky

1. bone
2. glove
3. wink
4. bird
5. feather
6. mule
7. bee
8. board

page 119

1. M
2. M
3. S
4. M
5. S

Tick-tock, tick-tock. Hannah bounced back and forth from one foot to the other, a clock counting down the seconds. She raised her racket and smacked the ball, sending it across the net like a rocket blasting through space.

Quickly, Hannah dashed to center court and waited, knees slightly bent. She was a lioness waiting patiently in the tall grass for her prey to come bounding back over the net. Hannah's opponent swung at the flying ball. His racket made a perfect arc around his body like a tetherball tied to a pole. He connected with the ball and turned it into yellow lightning that streaked back in the other direction.

In a flash, Hannah leaped to her left as suddenly as if some giant hand had yanked her sideways. She cranked her arm backward, setting the spring on a powerful catapult that sent the ball flying away from her.

The ball ricocheted between the two opponents for the next few minutes. The court echoed with a sound like popcorn popping in slow motion. Finally, Hannah directed the tennis ball to the far-left corner. Her opponent ran but arrived just in time to see it bounce away, a bus pulling from the curb with its doors closed.

"Good game, Dad!" Hannah yelled across the net.

page 120

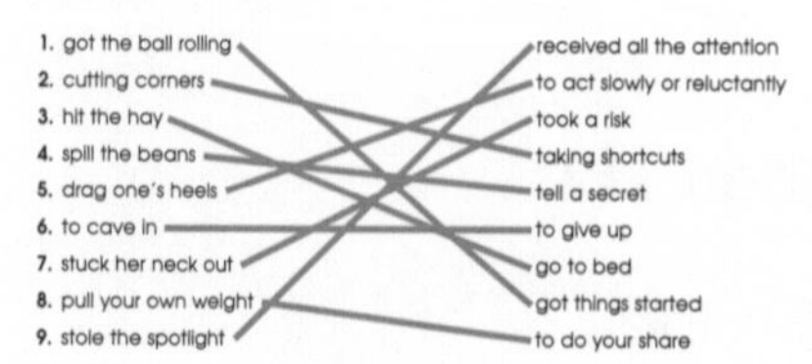

1. green thumb
2. know the ropes
3. lemon
4. skating on thin ice
5. horsing around
6. all thumbs
7. let the cat out of the bag

page 121

Answers will vary. Possible answers:

1. Henry was able to read between the lines and see what his coach really meant.
2. Mom was proud that Britta had stood her ground and stayed true to herself.
3. " I know it's going to be hard," Tanya told her group, "but it looks like we're going to have to go back to square one and see where the mistake is."
4. I was worried the test would be hard, but it was a piece of cake.
5. The new sports equipment cost an arm and a leg, but Zachary knew it was worth it.
6. The construction noise from across the street is beginning to get on my nerves.
7. Grace had been practicing for a week and knew the song backward and forward.

1. read; even
2. one's; easy

page 122
1. ugly
2. evening
3. children
4. state
5. Apple
6. seven
7. roar
8. dog

1. Answers will vary.
2. Answers will vary.

page 123
1. bake
2. messy
3. King
4. dollar
5. flower
6. time
7. kissing
8. Jazz

1. north
2. pool
3. bell
4. doctor
5. butterfly
6. ear

page 124
1. A chef cooks as an author writes.
2. Neigh is the sound a horse makes as meow is the sound a cat makes.
3. A yolk is inside an egg as a core is inside an apple.
4. Boring and exciting are antonyms as cheap and expensive are antonyms.
5. Pair and pear are homophones as serial and cereal are homophones.
6. A second is a portion of a minute as an ounce is a portion of a pound.

1. tight
2. Katherine
3. Cold
4. hive
5. eighteen
6. increase
7. Key
8. flock

page 125
1. thermometer; scale
2. Bat; golfer
3. pencil; delete
4. Monday; September
5. Smile; frown
6. Hammer; needle
7. freezing; hot
8. government; school
9. Conductor; basketball team
10. Money; knowledge

page 126
1. Homesickness washed over Maddy like a wave; S; homesickness and wave
2. Carter was a monkey; M; Carter and monkey
3. tongue feel like a big wad of cotton; S; tongue and wad of cotton
4. the classroom became as hot as an oven; S; classroom and oven
5. Mars looked like a tiny red marble; S; Mars and tiny red marble
6. Life is a journey; M; life and journey
7. backyard was transformed into a magical wonderland; M; backyard and magical wonderland

1. Answers will vary.
2. Answers will vary.
3. Answers will vary.
4. Answers will vary.

page 127
1. h
2. c
3. g
4. i
5. a
6. d
7. f
8. b
9. e

1. woman
2. star
3. tame
4. racket
5. fantastic
6. grasshopper
7. help
8. summer

page 128
sage * sandpaper
saleswoman
saliva
sandal

legislation * library
lemon
lesson

Answer Key

leotard
lengthwise

1–7. Answers will vary.

page 129
1. a
2. b
3. b
4. a
5. b
6. b
7. a
8. a
9. b
10. a
11. b

page 130
1. mayonnaise
2. locomotive
3. husky
4. beaver

1. 3
2. mysteries
3. Answers will vary. Possible answers: Daniel floundered with the packages for a minute before he was able to open the door. Would you rather have flounder, halibut, or salmon for dinner?
4. the first
5. no

page 131
isolate; resident; descendant; work; family; live; wide; quilt; recognize; attract; impress; inventive; create; display; stitch; woman; generation

page 132
1. b
2. a
3. a
4. c
5. b
6. a
7. c
8. b
9. a
10. b
11. b
12. a
13. c
14. b
15. a

<u>newscast * nimble</u>
nightingale
nickel
newsstand

<u>ninety * nook</u>
noise
nomination
noodle

<u>noon * notation</u>
north
nosebleed
nosy

page 133

			p											n	
			l									h		u	
			u								w	a	l	t	z
			g	o	o	s	e					p		t	
						t						p		y	
					f	r	i	e	n	d	l	y			
						a							a		
			e			i			c	l	o	u	d	y	
			c			g							o		
			h			h							r		
k	i	l	o	m	e	t	e	r					e		

1. the second
2. the second
3. noun
4. digest

page 134
Answers will vary. Possible answers:
1. friend, friendlier, friendliest, friendship, friends
2. rude, ruder, rudest, rudeness
3. erupt, erupts, erupting, eruption
4. appear, appears, appearing, disappear, disappeared, appearance, reappear
5. clean, cleans, cleaned, cleaning, cleanness, cleanly
6. spot, spots, spotted, spotting, spotty
7. deep, deeper, deepest, deepness, deepen
8. sweet, sweets, sweeter, sweetest, sweeten, sweetness, sweetly

page 135
1. a
2. c
3. b
4. a
5. a
6. c
7. a
8. c
9. b

1. Possible answers: consciousness,

Answer Key

consciously, subconscious, consciousness/ expectation, graduation, nationally, nations, international

2. playground; postgraduate; graduation; graduates

page 136

unmoving; snowflakes; skiwear; skis; snowy; removed; snowcapped; skied; moved; snowstorm; snowfall; skiing; moving; removable; skier; snowshoes; snowing; snowsuit; movement; moves; snowdrifts

<u>move</u>	<u>snow</u>
unmoving	snowflakes
removed	snowy
moved	snowcapped
moving	snowstorm
removable	snowfall
movement	snowshoes
moves	snowing
	snowsuit
	snowdrifts

<u>ski</u>
skiwear
skis
skied
skiing
skier

page 137

Possible answers:

<u>cover</u>	<u>joy</u>
covered	enjoy
covering	joyful
discover	joyfully
discovered	joyfulness
discovering	enjoying
uncover	enjoyed
uncovered	joyous
uncovering	joyously
recover	joyless
recovered	joylessly
recovering	rejoice
coverage	rejoicing

<u>create</u>
creating
created
creation
creator
recreate
recreated
recreating
recreation
creative
uncreative
creativity
creativeness

1. speakability
2. prewatched
3. valuelessly
4. unreading
5. unknowabled
6. malinformed
7. disinflamed
8. managist
9. foldness
10. needlessier
11. unbehavely
12. hearingly
13. restabled
14. speciallessly

page 138

1. h
2. l
3. j
4. i
5. a
6. b
7. c
8. d
9. k
10. e
11. g
12. f

page 139

1. phon
2. ann
3. geo
4. ped
5. meter
6. therm
7. liber
8. aqua
9. phon
10. ped

page 140

1. to move something from one place to another — transport
2. a star-shaped symbol on a computer keyboard — asterisk
3. to tell about or give details about something — describe
4. to send to another country for trade — export
5. a book written about a person's life — biography
6. to stop or break into something, like a conversation — interrupt
7. the study of stars — astronomy
8. something, such as a book, that is written — manuscript

i	k	v	h	w	e	b	i	o	g	r	a	p	h	y
n	r	h	n	s	p	p	r	e	m	m	s	t	q	a
t	q	m	a	n	u	s	c	r	i	p	t	p	k	s
e	p	e	h	n	f	f	u	r	e	q	r	h	r	t
r	t	g	t	u	i	m	e	a	x	g	o	v	d	e
r	i	d	e	u	p	l	r	t	p	b	n	f	a	r
u	t	w	r	b	d	y	w	e	o	r	o	h	d	i
p	t	t	r	a	n	s	p	o	r	t	m	l	o	s
t	d	e	s	c	r	i	b	e	t	e	y	b	b	k

page 141

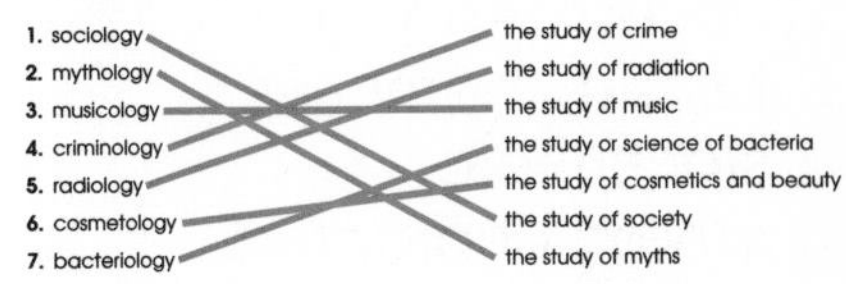

1. the study of the heart
2. the study of the mind

Answer Key

3. the study of birds
4. the study of the skin
5. the study of the universe
6. the study reptiles

1. myths, mythology
2. crime, criminology, music, bacteria, cosmetology, bacteriology, musicology, cosmetics

page 142

1. helpless, helpful
2. care, careful
3. performing, performance
4. irresponsible, responsible
5. unsuccessful, success
6. refreshments, fresh
7. history, historic

page 143

1. h
2. k
3. m
4. c
5. b
6. l
7. g
8. a
9. d
10. e
11. n
12. i
13. j
14. f

page 144

1. novelist; known
2. based; memories
3. story; there
4. similar; character; tomboy
5. fictional; love

page 145

1. pleasure
2. plume
3. pencil
4. cause
5. bizarre
6. oatmeal
7. weather

1. /niknām/
2. /lōkātəd/
3. /əfishəl/
4. /sīnd/
5. /popūlāshən/
6. /chikədē/
7. /ârēəz/
8. /sivəl/

page 146

largest; country; population; reach; any; foreign; Russians; urged; purchase; Although; citizens; nation; beautiful; millions; acres; destruction; economy; industries

page 147

1. ō
2. oi, oy
3. pierce, fear
4. u̇
5. rule, cool
6. a, e, i, o, u

1. Saturn
2. astronaut
3. launch
4. asteroid
5. laboratory
6. cockpit
7. satellite
8. atmosphere
9. spacecraft

astronaut, launch

page 148

1. a
2. a
3. b
4. a
5. b
6. a
7. b
8. a
9. a

1. zish
2. in
3. här
4. ôp
5. rith
6. duk

page 149

The ukulele may not be the most **/pop′ ye ler/** instrument, but as soon as most **/pē′ pel/** hear it, they love its **/plez′ ent/** sound. The Hawaiian ukulele, which looks like a small guitar, was modeled on a **/sim′ e ler/** Portuguese instrument brought to **/he wī′ ē/** in the 1870s. **/ôl thō′/** the ukulele had its **/grā′ test/ /pop′ ye lâr′ i tē/** in the 1920s, it has **/rē′ sent lē/** been enjoying a new surge in **/in′ trist/**. One good **/rē′ zen/** for this may be Jake Shimabukuro.

Jake was born and raised in Hawaii, where his **/muth′ er/** gave him his first ukulele lesson when he was **/ōn′ lē/** four years old. He has great respect for traditional ukulele **/myū′ zik/**, but Jake also **/en joiz′/** showing the world just how much the ukulele can do. His music **/ken tänz′/** elements of many **/dif′ er ent/** styles of music, **/in klū′ ding/** jazz, **/blū′ gras′/**, classical, and rock. As he strums and plucks the ukulele, his fingers move so fast, they're hard to follow. He makes it **/ē′ zē/** to **/un′ der stand′/** why the name *ukulele* is Hawaiian for *jumping flea*!

Some multiple-meaning words are spelled the same but pronounced differently. For example, present can be pronounced /pri zent′/ or /prez′ ent/. The meaning changes depending on the pronunciation and on the stress. Read each sentence below. Circle the respelling that shows how the bold word is used in the sentence.

1. The winner of the **contest** will receive a new bike. /kôn′ test′/ (circled) /ken test′/
2. My dad found his favorite old **record** online. /rek′ erd/ (circled) /ri kȯrd′/
3. *CD* is an acronym for ***compact*** *disk*. /kem pakt′/ /kôm′ pakt/ (circled)

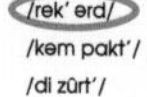

4. Many plants are found only in the **desert**. /di zûrt′/ /dez′ ert/ (circled)

page 150

/out dȯrz′/; /di rek′ sh ənz/; /trī/; /ak tiv′ i tē/; /smôl/; /spesh′ əl/; /sis′ təm/; /kum′ pəs/; /hid′ n/; /thēz/; /trezh′ er/; /bu̇k/; /men′ ē/;

/ēch/; /ri kȯrd′/;
/kôm′ entz/; /tāk/;
/sum′ thing/; /ī dē′ ə/;
/duz′ ənz/; /mīt/; /wu̇d/

1. b
2. a
3. a
4. b
5. b
6. a

page 151

/vin′ i gər/; /clā/; /sō′ də/

1. /pōk/; /in sûrt′/;
   /ə round′/
2. /pēs/; /kâr′ fə lē/;
   /pri vent′/; /sek′ əndz/
4. /wô′ tər/; /bi nēth′/; /līk/;
   /mō′ tər/
5. /kwik′ lē/
6. /hwen/; /rē akt′/;
   /kär′ bən/

Notes

Notes

Notes

Notes

Notes

Notes